# PHILOSOPHY OF RELIGION SERIES

## *Editor's Note*

The philosophy of religion is one of several very active branches of philosophy today, and the present series is designed both to consolidate the gains of the past and to direct attention upon the problems of the future. Between them these volumes will cover every aspect of the subject, introducing it to the reader in the state in which it is today, including its open ends and growing points. Thus the series is designed to be used as a comprehensive textbook for students. But it is also offered as a contribution to present-day discussion; and each author will accordingly go beyond the scope of an introduction to formulate his own position in the light of contemporary debates.

JOHN HICK

Philosophy of Religion Series

General Editor: John Hick, H. G. Wood Professor of Theology,
University of Birmingham


Published
*John Hick (Birmingham University) Arguments
for the Existence of God*
*H. P. Owen (King's College, London) Concepts of Deity*
*Kai Nielsen (Calgary University)*
*Contemporary Critiques of Religion*
*Terence Penelhum (Calgary University)*
*Problems of Religious Knowledge*
*M. J. Charlesworth (Melbourne University)*
*Philosophy of Religion: The Historic Approaches*
*William A. Christian (Yale University) Oppositions of Religious Doctrines:
A Study in the Logic of Dialogue among Religions*


Forthcoming titles
*Ninian Smart (Lancaster University) The Phenomenon of Religion*
*Basil Mitchell (Oriel College, Oxford)*
*The Language of Religion*
*Nelson Pike (California University)*
*Religious Experience and Mysticism*
*Donald Evans (Toronto University) Religion and Morality*
*Dennis Nineham (Keble College, Oxford) Faith and History*
*H. D. Lewis (King's College, London) The Self and Immortality*

# OPPOSITIONS OF RELIGIOUS DOCTRINES

A Study in the Logic of Dialogue among Religions

WILLIAM A. CHRISTIAN

MACMILLAN

*First published 1972 by*
THE MACMILLAN PRESS LTD
*London and Basingstoke*
*Associated companies in New York Toronto*
*Dublin Melbourne Johannesburg and Madras*

SBN 333 07903 5

*Printed in Great Britain by*
WESTERN PRINTING SERVICES LTD
*Bristol*

For R. G. C.

# Contents

# Acknowledgements

Along with the debts I have mentioned in the text I owe a great deal to the students and faculty of the Department of Religious Studies of this university, especially to my colleagues Judah Goldin, Sid Leiman, Jaroslav Pelikan and Stanley Weinstein. They were patient with my naïve questions and generous with their knowledge. Professor William H. Austin of Rice University and William A. Christian Jr read parts of the manuscript and made helpful comments. Over many years I have learned much from Norvin Hein.

WILLIAM A. CHRISTIAN

Timothy Dwight College
Yale University
April 1971

# 1 Introduction

In the past two centuries and a half several developments have increased the likelihood of serious conversations about doctrines among proponents of different religions. Among these developments are the scholarly study of the literatures and histories of religions, missionary movements from West to East and from East to West, and a general lifting of cultural horizons. It is still unlikely that these conversations will occur very often because scholarly study encourages one to speak from a detached point of view rather than as a proponent of a religion, because missionary enterprises have built-in limitations as well as possibilities for serious give-and-take in discussions, and because world-minded people often take the bland view that differences in doctrine do not really matter. Moreover, the conditions of success in conducting these conversations, that is for bringing about genuine meetings of minds, persistent explorations of issues and vigorous arguments, are difficult to satisfy.

Even so philosophers, especially philosophers of religion, should be interested in the logic and the ethics of these conversations, just as anthropologists, psychologists and sociologists should be interested in the habits which condition them. This essay is a study in their logic, concentrating on one particular topic, namely how oppositions of doctrines of different religions are possible.

There are oppositions of concepts (e.g., up/down, good/bad) (1), oppositions of persons (contestants, enemies), and oppositions of institutions (religions, nations, political parties). We are not directly concerned with these oppositions but with oppositions of doctrines. Not with oppositions of concepts, expressed by contrasting terms, for oppositions of doctrines have to be expressed by contrasting sentences; not with oppositions of persons, though some moral problems are touched on briefly; and not with oppositions of religions as historically concrete social systems firmly

1

ensconced in particular cultural settings, but only with one element in such systems, namely their doctrines.

Following the lead of the dictionary a doctrine of a religious community is something 'which is taught or set forth for acceptance or belief' by that community. Since a religion teaches a pattern of life, not just a view of the world, some of its doctrines will say what one ought to do, inwardly and outwardly, while others will say what the world is like. So the force of some utterances of doctrines is to recommend courses of action; others have the force of assertions. Hence when we come to ask how doctrines can be opposed, part of the answer will turn out to be: not in one way only.

Two doctrines are opposed if they cannot be accepted jointly without absurdity. To accept a doctrine which recommends a course of action is to undertake to do what is recommended. So two such doctrines are opposed if no one could undertake both courses of action without absurdity. To accept a doctrine conveyed in an assertion is to take what is asserted as true. (The question arises in Chapter 5 whether this should be qualified for assertions of valuations.) This includes being willing to assert it oneself in appropriate circumstances and to act on it if an occasion for doing so should arise. So two assertions are in opposition if it would be absurd to take both what is said in one and what is said in the other as true. Thus doctrines which assert something are opposed if they are contrary to one another or if they are contradictory of one another.

If one doctrine asserts something and another doctrine recommends some course of action, then the doctrines are opposed if it is not possible without absurdity both to take what the assertion says as true and to undertake to do what the other doctrine recommends. For example, it would be absurd for someone both (a) to believe it would be impossible to carry out some course of action and also (b) to undertake that course of action. And therefore it would be absurd for someone both (a) to say some course of action is impossible and (b) to recommend undertaking that course of action.

So there are oppositions of various kinds, and explanations of just how it would be absurd or inconsistent or indefensible to accept (and hence to propose) both of some pair of doctrines

2

would have to be different for different kinds of cases, as we shall see. We learn whether two doctrines are in opposition by looking at their forms, or by knowing conceptual structures, or by knowing how things are in the world, or by more than one of these ways.

Many oppositions of religious doctrines are internal to one or another particular religion. In these cases Buddhists disagree with other Buddhists about what should be counted as Buddhist doctrines, Christians disagree with other Christians about what the Church should teach, and similarly for the other religions. Should Buddhists say that the ideal of life is to become an arahat, as Theravada Buddhism has taught, or that the ideal is to become a bodhisattva at Mahayana Buddhism has taught? Should Christians say with the Baptists that, since the Church is a community of believers, those who are baptised into it should be able to make a confession of faith and hence infants should not be baptised? Or should they say with the Catholics and others that the Church is a more comprehensive body and that infants should be baptised as well as those who can confess their faith?

Disagreements and disputes about doctrines have occurred within each of the major religions. More often than not they are amicable and have no serious practical consequences, but sometimes they tend to disrupt the life of the community and threaten to destroy its unity. Hence a religious community has to find ways of dealing with internal oppositions of doctrines. Theologians (and their equivalents in non-theistic religions) may be able to mitigate or reconcile them by reformulations of the doctrines of the community. Or a consensus may develop in favour of one of the opposed doctrines and against the other. In any case these internal oppositions are a spur to that process of formulating and developing doctrines which is part of the life of a religious community throughout its history. These are problems for the community itself to solve.

Disagreements within a religious tradition have to be settled, in as far as they can be settled, in accord with principles which are inherent in the tradition itself, by appeal to sacred scriptures, to the practice of revered teachers and to the generally approved habits of life and thought within the community. This necessity of common principles in dealing with internal oppositions is

3

reflected in the following passage from Augustine's argument against the Arian bishop Maximinus. Just before this Augustine has alluded to the Council of Nicaea but, he says:

> I ought not to bring forward the Council of Nicaea, nor should you bring forward the Council of Ariminum, as a way of deciding the issue beforehand. I am not bound by the authority of the latter, and you are not bound by the authority of the former. Instead let our concerns, arguments and convictions contend with one another by reference to the authoritative witnesses of the scriptures, which do not belong exclusively to either side but are common to both. ('Cont. Max.' II xiv 3; Migne, PL 42, col. 772)

We will not have our eye on these internal oppositions, on disagreements among Hindus or among Buddhists or among Jews or among Christians or among Muslims. Instead our topic is oppositions of doctrines of different religions and hence the disagreements which might arise between a Hindu and a Muslim, or between a Buddhist and a Jew. (Also we leave out disagreements between proponents of some religion and non-religious sceptics or positivists.)

Oppositions of doctrines of different religions could not be settled in the ways appropriate to internal oppositions. Even when two traditions overlap historically and share some habits of thought as Hinduism and Buddhism do, and even when they have some scriptures in common as Judaism and Christianity do, their principles of judgement are by no means the same. Christians do not interpret what they call the Old Testament in the same way Jews do. Indeed, the fact that they call this collection of books the 'Old Testament', in contrast with the New Testament, illustrates the point.

So principles of judgement for these external oppositions are more problematical than those for internal oppositions (2). In many cases no equivalent of Augustine's appeal to the Bible is available. And this means that external oppositions are themselves more problematical than internal ones. For if there were no principles of judgement at all, could a contrast of doctrines have the logical force of an opposition? Perhaps, one might think

4

in that case, the disagreements are only reflections of contrasting styles of life analogous to contrasting styles of dress or painting or music.

On the face of it this is not plausible. Generally religious people do not behave as though differences of religions were just matters of taste. Current debates between proponents of different religions, for example Buddhists and Christians (3), clearly suppose that genuine oppositions of doctrines are involved. Also, commonly we feel strong resistance to saying of anyone that he is both a good Muslim and a good Episcopalian, or both a good Hindu and a good Buddhist. The reasons for this resistance are no doubt complex, some of them being our associations of certain religions with particular nationalities and styles of culture, but among these reasons there are also feelings that there is something logically wrong about saying things like this, because we suppose that accepting both sets of doctrines would involve an absurdity.

Conceivably this prevalent supposition, that some doctrines of different religions are indeed opposed to one another, might turn out to be untenable. Conceivably the doctrines of the major religions are all consistent with one another. It might even be that, rightly understood, they all say the same thing. When we study the history of religions these latter views do seem very implausible, and certainly much current talk in aid of these views is loose and sentimental. One wants to say, in response to the generous impulses which often prompt people to harmonise the doctrines of the world religions, that understanding one another does not always lead to agreement and that respect for one another does not depend on agreement. Still, if one does not accept these views then arguments against them are called for.

Though I believe there are indeed genuine oppositions of doctrines of different religions, I do not propose to argue that case in this essay; at least I shall not give a complete argument for it. I shall try to show something short of that, namely how such oppositions are possible. This fails to be a complete argument for the existence of oppositions of doctrines of different religions in the following way. Suppose that one finds certain sentences $s$ and $s'$ in the literatures of different religions, or that $s$ and $s'$ are strongly suggested by what one reads in those literatures or by what one hears from adherents of those religions. And suppose

5

further that one could succeed in showing that what would be said in an utterance of $s$, when the utterance occurs in a certain kind of situation, is indeed opposed to what would be said in an utterance of $s'$ in that same kind of situation. To show that we would have here an opposition of doctrines of different religions, one would have to go further and argue that these utterances of $s$ and of $s'$ do indeed truly state doctrines of those religions.

There are several reasons why I do not propose to make and argue claims of this last sort. (It would be bootless to make them without arguing for them.) One is that this would complicate the enterprise enormously, even if I knew a great deal more about the history of religions than I do. To show how oppositions of doctrines of different religions are possible is quite enough to undertake in a small essay, without setting out to show that certain formulations, vis-à-vis alternative formulations, do well and truly state doctrines of Hinduism or of Buddhism or of Christianity, for example. That would require surveys of the histories of those traditions, as well as appeals to what is said by those who can speak for them with some authority at the present time. Also it would require decisions of my own in doubtful cases, and that leads me to a second reason for limiting the argument to showing how external oppositions are possible.

If some religion $R$ which we are studying is a living and growing tradition, not just a set of institutions which existed in the past, it must have the final word on what its doctrines are. We have to distinguish between (i) assertions of the form 'It is a doctrine of $R$ that $p$' and (ii) assertions of $p$, for these are very different. It would be consistent for someone to say both that $p$ is indeed a doctrine of $R$ and that $p$ is not true. Someone, for example a Jew or a Muslim, might well agree that it is a doctrine of the Christian Church that God is a Trinity without agreeing to the doctrine of the Trinity. At the moment I am calling attention to assertions of type (i), to the effect that some formulation truly states a doctrine of a certain religion. If a religion is a living tradition it has the right to speak for itself when these assertions are in question and to tell us what its own doctrines are.

The point is not that only the members of a religious community can understand its doctrines. I am not arguing that; indeed I believe it is not true. My point is a different one. The

6

difficulty I am pointing to is not about understanding what is being said in some formulation one finds in the literature of some religion, though of course there are plenty of difficulties about that; the issue is whether what is being said amounts to a doctrine of that religion, or whether, for example, it is only a permitted opinion.

Very often there are differences of judgement within a community about what its doctrines are. Different formulations of doctrines are put forward. This takes us back to the internal oppositions of doctrines we were noticing earlier. Then the issue is: which of these formulations are more faithful to the tradition and the spirit of the religion? This is the issue which must be settled from within the community if it can be settled at all. More often than not there are no dramatic settlements of these issues, for example by a decision of a council, and even the decision of a council may not settle the issue for all time. On many such issues different convictions continue to be expressed and are subject to the test of time, as in the parable of the wheat and the tares. The point I would stress is the kind of issue which is involved in these cases and the kind of claim that is being made in assertions of the form '$p$ is a doctrine of $R$'.

One might say that these are theological issues rather than philosophical issues, except that 'theological' suggests theism and hence does not clearly apply to all of the religious traditions. My object is to confine my own argument to philosophical issues as far as I can.

Scholars who do not adhere to some religion can study its literature and its history and contribute to our knowledge of them. They may even try to sum up and systematise what its doctrines were in the past, remote or recent. George Foot Moore's 'Judaism' (4) is a case in point. But even a very great scholar might be sensible of trepidation if he should be tempted to say not only what has been normative for a religion in the past but what ought to be normative for its life today and in the future, if he is not himself in a position to speak for that community. Certainly, however sympathetic and friendly his viewpoint might be, one would still want to hear from those who can speak for the community itself, whose lives and thought have been shaped by its tradition, when *that* question is at issue. Knowledge of what the

7

tradition has amounted to in the past is not enough, for if it is indeed a living and growing tradition its past will condition but not determine its present and its future.

So I shall develop some formulations suggested to me by the literatures of different religions, to use as working examples. I propose to show how certain inferences might be drawn from them, and thus to show how oppositions of different kinds might occur. I shall hope that proponents of those religions will not find these formulations too implausible to be useful for my purpose. But my aim is not a historical one, and certainly I do not undertake to tell any religious community what its doctrines are or what they ought to be. I ask only how oppositions of doctrines of different religions are possible, and my conclusions will be hypothetical in the following way. Suppose it can be shown that some $p$ and some $q$, which are at least plausible candidates for being doctrines of religions $R^1$ and $R^2$ respectively, are opposed. Then *if* $p$ does indeed count as a doctrine of $R^1$, and the same for $q$ and $R^2$, then a doctrine of $R^1$ and a doctrine of $R^2$ are opposed. Conclusions which remain hypothetical in this way should be enough to show how doctrines of different religions might be opposed to one another.

In this essay we study a limited topic in the critical philosophy of religion so, to get the topic in perspective, we should consider what goes on in critical philosophy of religion and then see the place of this topic in that enterprise. Critical philosophy (in something like Kant's sense of 'critical') in so far as it can be distinguished from speculative philosophy, normative ethics and other philosophical undertakings, studies:

(*a*) the principles of judgement employed in various domains of inquiry and discourse (e.g., perceptual experience, the natural sciences, morality, law, religion, aesthetic experience);

(*b*) general conditions of truth or validity or acceptability, common to the various domains;

(*c*) how the principles of judgement in various domains specify the general conditions; and

(*d*) the patterns of relatedness (connections, analogies) which hold between different domains, or between types of utterances in different domains of discourse.

8

So critical philosophy of religion as a branch of critical philosophy is a different enterprise from religious philosophy, in which religious individuals develop their own religious convictions and reflections in a philosophical manner. It is different also from the active development of the doctrines of some religious community. (Unfortunately there is no handy term to abbreviate 'the development of doctrines in some religious community or other', since 'theology' fits only theistic religions.) But it is not in principle inimical to either of these other enterprises. It begins with what religious people say, taken in connection with what they do, much as critical philosophy of science begins with what scientists say in connection with what they do, and studies the concepts, the recommendations and claims, and the arguments which are distinctive in religious discourse. Another parallel with philosophy of science, and with critical philosophy in other domains, is that as a rule we fail to see the point and the force of a doctrine if we have no acquaintance with its setting in religious life.

Critical philosophy of religion is a relatively young discipline and it is still very much in process of development. It goes back to the beginnings of the critical study of religion as a kind of human experience and activity, which got under way in the seventeenth and eighteenth centuries. Spinoza's 'Tractatus Theologico-Politicus' (1670) is an early landmark in this phase, anticipating Kant's 'Religion within the Limits of Reason Alone' by more than a hundred years. But not much real progress could be made without reliable knowledge of a fairly wide range of religions, which began to accumulate only in the nineteenth century. For when philosophers were not forced to take account of the plurality of religious traditions in more than a peripheral manner, problems of critical philosophy of religion tended to get confused with theological problems. For example, one might easily be tempted to take Spinoza's 'Tractatus' and Kant's 'Religion' as contributions to Christian theology, though this would not be the only way and certainly not the fairest way to judge them.

In this century two developments within critical philosophy of religion are particularly relevant and noteworthy. One is to take seriously the plurality of religious traditions including Eastern religions, as for example Rudolf Otto does in 'Mysticism East and West' (5) and as Ninian Smart does in 'Reasons and Faiths'

(6). This is a healthy development because then it becomes much easier to distinguish the problems of critical philosophy of religion from those involved in the development of doctrines in some religious community, and for another reason as well. It puts the problems of natural theology into a wider critical perspective. These perennial problems have been discussed in new and illuminating ways by theistic and anti-theistic philosophers in recent years, but it would be unfortunate if philosophy of religion should come to be simply identified with natural theology.

Another development, which has gained ground in the past generation, is to approach critical problems by considering the character and structure of religious discourse. It is often pointed out that the study of discourse is not an altogether new tack in philosophy, and certainly it is not a cure-all for philosophical problems, but it has advantages for some topics and particularly for our own. Various ways of interpreting religious discourse have been tried. Some years ago it was not uncommon for philosophers to interpret and measure religious discourse by models derived from perceptual discourse or scientific discourse. Those models did not succeed well in capturing the most distinctive features of religious discourse. In more recent years, under the influence of the later Wittgenstein other approaches are more common. But these often have the effect of isolating religion from other modes of experience in an unreal way. I shall not try to develop a more adequate general theory of religious discourse in this essay, certainly not in a systematic way. At this point in the development of critical philosophy of religion it may be time to explore more limited topics.

Our own limited topic, philosophical study of oppositions of doctrines of different religions, has only a short and meagre history, though the history of its subject-matter extends far back into ancient times. Cases where a proponent of one religion argues against doctrines of another religion have long been familiar in the history of religions. Examples are to be found in the second-century Buddhist treatise, 'The Questions of King Milinda'; Justin Martyr's 'Dialogue with Trypho' and the writings of other early church fathers; and the tenth-century treatise by the Jewish philosopher Saadia Gaon, 'The Book of Beliefs and Opinions' (7). The main object in these treatises is to present

10

arguments for one faith and against others. So by and large these are not antecedents of this study but only a part of its subject-matter.

Furthermore, religions which propose their doctrines to outsiders and defend them have had to develop some guiding principles for doing so. For example, the following deal with problems of Christian apologetics: Leonard Hodgson, 'The Place of Reason in Christian Apologetic' (1925); Hendrik Kraemer, 'The Christian Message in a Non-Christian World' (1938) and 'Religion and the Christian Faith' (1956). These apologetic principles of various religions also bear on our topic, but again I confess I have not found such treatises of great help in philosophical analysis of oppositions, though they are an interesting part of the subject-matter of the problem.

The direct antecedents of this essay, from which I have received most help in formulating and exploring its problems, are quite recent. Mentioning some of these may help to show the general orientation of the essay, even though they do not undertake to do just what it aims to do.

Rudolf Otto's 'The Idea of the Holy' (8) has been taken by its readers in various ways – as a study in the phenomenology of religion, as an essay in religious philosophy with idealistic suppositions, and perhaps most often as a contribution to Christian theology. Doubtless it exhibits all these intentions and that is one reason for a number of confusions in interpreting it. It is also an essay in critical philosophy, aiming to show what is distinctive in religious concepts and judgements, a post-Kantian critique of religious judgement. I believe that its philosophical importance is mainly due to this intention, which is not carried out very thoroughly or systematically, it is true, but with more sensitivity to varieties of religious experience and more philosophical acuteness than it has been given credit for. It is still a good starting-point for investigation of the logic of religious discourse.

'Reasons and Faiths' by Ninian Smart is the most original study of the logical structure of religious doctrines since Otto, and on the whole it is more philosophically acute. His conceptual framework is more fundamentally and consistently shaped with a view to comparative study than Otto's, and he is more explicitly concerned with oppositions of doctrines. He argues there are

11

various 'logical strands' in religious discourse, reflecting different types of religious experience. Assertions that something or other is holy, in Otto's sense, belong to one of these strands. But there are other strands. (As Otto himself comes close to saying in 'Mysticism East and West' (9), a comparative study of Shankara and Eckhart.) So Smart is in a better position to do justice to the complex structures of doctrinal schemes, and to contrasts and oppositions between doctrines belonging to different schemes. In 'A Dialogue of Religions' (10) Smart constructs a dialogue to exhibit various lines of argument which would be appropriate in conversations among proponents of different religious traditions.

J. M. Bochenski, O.P., in 'The Logic of Religion' (11) includes in the scope of logic both semiotics and methodology (theory of truth-conditions) as well as formal logic. Like Smart he is not speaking as a theologian; he does not purport to assert or justify any one religious doctrine rather than another. He means to develop a theory which applies to more than one religion, indeed 'to all great religions' (vi). He is less concerned than Smart with analysis of particular religious doctrines and doctrinal schemes, and more concerned (at least more explicitly so) to apply general logical principles to religious discourse. He does not explicitly consider oppositions of doctrines of different religions, though much that he says is suggestive.

This essay is much more narrowly focused than the studies I have just mentioned; its topic is a smaller one. Yet a study of this topic could contribute significantly to the critical philosophy of religion, that is to say to an understanding of the logic of religious discourse, and some indication of this is in order before we go further, to suggest some of the possibilities which go along with the limitations of the study.

Often we make discoveries about the logic of religious discourse in the following way. One makes what seems a relevant objection $(q)$ to some doctrine $(p)$, only to find that the proponent of $p$ disallows the objection because he regards $q$ either as irrelevant to the point of $p$ or as not inconsistent with $p$. So it seems that he is operating with different rules for relevance and consistency than one had supposed. This disconcerting experience must be familiar to anyone who has tried to understand an alien scheme of religious doctrines, but often it is the way we learn something new.

12

There is nothing peculiar to religion in this; the same kind of thing happens with legal doctrines, scientific doctrines, and others. For example, the Declaration of Independence says that all men are created equal. Now if someone objected that there are biological inequalities among men, the founding fathers might well have said this missed the point, that the doctrine is a moral claim which has important applications precisely because of biological and other inequalities. In general, what is being said in the utterance of some doctrine depends on the rules by which its concepts operate, and often we find what these are by trying out objections.

So one way we could learn the rules of relevance and consistency of some scheme of religious doctrines would be to see what oppositions it countenances and hence what objections its proponents can admit. This study does not purport to explore the logic of any particular religion as understood by its proponents, for reasons I have explained. It does explore some of the types of possible oppositions which might be tried out in the dialectical process of coming to learn the logic of some doctrinal scheme in discussion with its proponents.

Some theologians (and their equivalents in non-theistic religions) seem to say that the only relevant objections to their doctrines are those from within the tradition. Then the only oppositions such a theologian will countenance would be of the form: $p$, not $q$, is true to the tradition/$q$, not $p$, is true to the tradition. The issue between Augustine and Maximinus was of this kind. The tradition itself provides rules for judging such issues, and these rules are necessary and sufficient though they may not be easy to apply.

Now if no other oppositions could be admitted (which was certainly not the case for Augustine), this would tell us something important about the theologian's claims. It would tell us that his claims do not extend beyond the boundaries of his own religious community. The rule would be: Muslim doctrines are only for Muslims; Buddhist doctrines are only for Buddhists; and so on.

Suppose, however, that the proponent of a doctrine admits objections advanced by members of other religious communities speaking as such, thus countenancing oppositions between his doctrine and doctrines of other religions. This would tell us some-

13

thing different about the claim he is making and the rules which govern what he says. In this event he is extending his claim beyond his own community and not all of his rules are peculiar to his own tradition.

Suppose a speaker admits, along with internal objections and objections from other religious traditions, objections based on perceptual experience or historical inquiry or natural science or speculative philosophy. Then he countenances oppositions between doctrines of his religion and non-religious doctrines and thus recognises some logical connections between religion and other domains.

Though we confine ourselves to oppositions of doctrines of different religions, the outcome may suggest how a wider study of oppositions could contribute to understanding the logic of religious discourse. It can teach us something about the kinds of claims made in religious utterances, the kinds of objections which are admitted as relevant, and the kinds of arguments which are required to support these claims.

It will be a healthy thing to remind ourselves that oppositions of doctrines have a secondary place in religious discourse. Though echoes of conflicts may resound in the very words of a prayer or a creed, for example 'There is no God but Allah', in most cases the main point of a religious utterance is not argumentative. In the standard settings of primary religious discourse disagreements and arguments about doctrines are of incidental importance, if any.

Instead hymns are sung, prayers and creeds are said, sacred scriptures are read and expounded. Stories are told of what happened in the Exodus from Egypt; of what the Buddha said and did; of the patriarchs of the tradition; of how Jesus brought personal salvation and happiness to the speaker; of Arjuna's encounter with Krishna before the battle; of a journey from the City of Destruction to the Heavenly City. Ways of life are explained. The roshi tells what it means to have the Zen experience and to be a Zen man; the swami speaks of the way to spiritual peace and freedom; the evangelist sets forth the requirements and the resources of the Christian life.

Though arguments are often implicit and even sometimes explicit in these utterances, their primary settings and intentions are not mainly governed by oppositions of doctrines, certainly not

14

by oppositions of doctrines of different religions. So the subject-matter of this essay should be viewed in proportion to its place in the total range of religious discourse. Two layers in the structure of religious discourse are involved here. First, the main point of the doctrines of a religion is not to deny the doctrines of other religions; they are not generated simply as negative reactions to doctrines of other religions. One could not understand the genesis and intentions and uses of the doctrines of a religion if one took them in that way. On the contrary, the main point of the doctrines of a religion is to say something positive about the meaning of life. Second, the doctrines of a religion themselves are generated by a certain vision of life, and this vision is suggested and shaped by particular experiences and practices in particular historical and social settings. Thus oppositions of doctrines are derivative and consequential; they are twice removed from those particular experiences and activities which are existentially primary in religion.

Showing that two doctrines are opposed would not be enough to show that one or the other must be true or valid or right. Even if we could show of some Hindu doctrine and some Christian doctrine that no one could accept both without absurdity, we could not conclude just from this that one is true and the other untrue. Both might be untrue. The doctrines might be contrary but not contradictory. The truth of the matter might turn out to be different from what is said in either.

It is surprisingly rare for a doctrine of one religion to contradict a doctrine of another religion explicitly. This is partly because, as I was suggesting earlier, the initial intentions of religious doctrines are not mainly polemical. A religion arises, develops and survives only if it has something positive to say about human life within the conditions of existence. It is also partly because some of the major religions developed in relative independence of one another historically speaking.

Furthermore, doctrines of different religions can differ from one another without being opposed to one another. And an opposition between two schemes of doctrine at one point does not necessarily mean there are oppositions at other points as well. The following passage from the Muslim theologian al-Ghazālī (1058–1111) puts this in an interesting way:

15

This is like a man who hears a Christian assert, 'There is no god but God, and Jesus is the Messenger of God.' The man rejects this, saying, 'This is a Christian conception,' and does not pause to ask himself whether the Christian is an infidel in respect of this assertion or in respect of his denial of the prophethood of Muhammad (peace be upon him). If he is an infidel only in respect of his denial of Muhammad, then he need not be contradicted in other assertions, true in themselves and not connected with his unbelief, even though these are also true in his eyes (12).

Are the doctrines of the major religions of the world really, in spite of their differences and even in spite of *prima facie* oppositions between them, consistent with one another? Or are they all really saying the same thing? Clearly the study will bear on these questions. Not because I shall argue that genuine oppositions do exist and that therefore the doctrines of the major religions are not consistent and cannot be saying the same thing. I do not undertake to do as much as that. It is only that if we can see some ways in which oppositions might occur we would be in a better position to judge, from a concrete knowledge of what particular religious traditions do actually teach, whether oppositions do actually occur. We can lay out some *kinds* of oppositions which, if anyone maintains that all religions are consistent with one another or that they say the same thing, would have to be shown to be only specious and not real.

# 2  A Model Situation

However it may be with other domains of discourse, when we study religious discourse we cannot disregard the situations in which sentences are spoken or written; we have to take account of utterances of sentences as well as sentences. Yet if we are interested in specific features of some range of discourse we need some way of highlighting those features, leaving others to one side as not immediately relevant to our purpose. With these considerations in mind I shall outline a hypothetical situation as a device for studying how oppositions between doctrines of different religions are possible.

Suppose a number of people are conversing in some common natural language and that the following conditions hold:

1. By conviction they belong to different religious communities; one is a Hindu, one is a Buddhist, and so on.

2. Each is reasonably well educated in the doctrines and practices of his own religion.

3. Each knows reasonably well the literatures and histories of the other religions. (This is to minimise impasses in conversation due to ignorance.)

4. Each is reasonably intelligent and acute. (To minimise impasses due to stupidity and obtuseness.)

5. They speak with candour and treat one another with respect and charity. (To minimise impasses due to defensiveness or malice.)

6. No one is present as an official representative of his own religious community. (To minimise official diplomacy, in reinforcement of 5.)

7. Each puts forward some doctrines of his religion for acceptance by the others and is ready and willing to give reasons for accepting the doctrines he proposes.

Situations like this are not the most common settings for

17

utterances of religious doctrines, but it is reasonably clear that doctrines are uttered in such situations sometimes and that there is nothing unnatural about this. It is not unnatural and certainly not unreasonable for human beings to be ready and willing to gain practical wisdom and to share it with others.

We want to see what can be said and what cannot be said in this model situation (S), but first some of its conditions need to be developed further, especially some implications of condition 7.

Because of condition 7, though exchanges of information about religious traditions (minimised by condition 2) may occur, the conversation in S cannot consist entirely of such utterances. In this way S differs from conferences of historians of religion or anthropologists or sociologists or psychologists or of mixtures of these such as the Society for the Scientific Study of Religion. In those gatherings someone might put forward some religious doctrine for acceptance by his colleagues but generally the circumstances discourage this, and it is not essential to those situations that any such proposals should be made.

S is different. It is essential to the situation that such utterances occur. To satisfy condition 7 it is not enough that Hindu beliefs and Buddhist beliefs, for example, are reported; it is necessary that some doctrines are asserted. Discourse in S is thus also different from what is said in a textbook for the comparative study of religion. The textbook needs to say such things, for example, as:

(i) Hinduism teaches that the self is eternal.
(ii) Buddhism teaches that all things are impermanent.

But in S things of the following sort would need to be said as well:

(iii) The self is eternal.
(iv) All things are impermanent.

Asserting that some religion teaches some doctrine is very different from asserting that doctrine. Different sorts of claims are being made in these different sorts of utterances.

Scholars who study the history and literature of Hinduism can disagree about what doctrines Hinduism teaches without asserting those doctrines. But the oppositions which would occur in

18

these disagreements would not be oppositions of religious doctrines. Also, Hindus can disagree among themselves about what Hinduism teaches, but this would not yield oppositions of doctrines of different religions.

This brings out the reason why we need condition 7 as well as condition 1 if we want a model situation for studying oppositions of doctrines of different religions. There is a *prima facie* opposition between (iii) and (iv), but there is no opposition between (i) and (ii), for (i) and (ii) are co-assertable and co-acceptable without any absurdity. Whether or not they happen to be true as a matter of fact, they are not inconsistent with one another. So the natural setting for our study is one in which doctrines of different religions are asserted; it is not enough for them to be reported.

This is a point about the force of an utterance, not about the form of words used in the utterance. Speakers in $S$ might well assert doctrines by saying something of the form 'We (Buddhists, e.g.) believe and teach that $d$' or 'I believe that $d$' or even 'It seems to me that $d$'.

This distinction between the force of an utterance and the form of words holds in the opposite direction too. The author of a history of Buddhism writes, 'When the third Dalai-lama died, he was reincarnated in the grandson of Altan Khan', but we do not take this as an assertion of the incarnation doctrine of the Yellow Sect of Tibetan Buddhism, especially when the next sentence says that this birth of the fourth Dalai-lama among the Mongols was probably the result of some intrigue! (1) When the author says the third Dalai-lama was reincarnated, this is a manner of speaking. We understand that he is telling us what the Buddhists of the Yellow Sect believed and taught.

Condition 7 does not insist on *blunt* assertions of doctrines. For normally we take first-person statements of belief as conveying implicit assertions of what is said to be believed. That is why the following conjunction of utterances would sound paradoxical:

(v) I believe that $p$. & It is not the case that $p$. (2)

When a speaker says something of the form 'I believe that $p$' we do not normally suppose that he is merely reporting some inner experience or state in an informative way, as he might

19

report a nightmare for example. There is nothing paradoxical about the following as there is about (v):

(vi) Often I have nightmares about green monsters, but of course there are no green monsters.

Nor do we ordinarily suppose that in utterances of the form 'I (we) believe that $p$' the speaker is merely presenting the sentence '$p$' to be entertained or contemplated. It is true that some philosophers have interpreted religious beliefs in a peculiar way. For example R. B. Braithwaite says:

> A religious assertion, . . is the assertion of an intention to carry out a certain behaviour policy . . . together with the implicit or explicit statement, but not the assertion, of certain stories . . . a religious belief is an intention to behave in a certain way (a moral belief) together with the entertainment of certain stories associated with the intention in the mind of the believer (3).

Braithwaite agrees that on this view 'belief' and 'assertion' come to have different meanings than they ordinarily do.

D. Z. Phillips, inspired by Wittgenstein's 1938 lectures on religious belief – as indeed Braithwaite may have been also – seems to give a somewhat similar sense to 'believe' in speaking of religious belief in the Last Judgement. He says this belief is not a conjecture about the future. For the believer it is 'as it were, the framework, the religious framework, within which he meets fortune, misfortune, and the evil that he finds in his own life and in life about him'. Certainly this sounds like a stronger attitude than entertainment. But he says that 'the believer's belief' does not include any reactions like 'I believe it is going to happen' (4). So he leaves the reader wondering whether the believer's belief includes any beliefs at all in the ordinary sense of belief. Hence, one wonders whether, as well as saying the belief is not a conjecture about the future, he would not be willing to say also it is not a conviction about the future either.

The immediate interest of these interpretations of religious belief is their bearing on the possibility of oppositions of religious doctrines, for they assign certain functions and not others to utterances of religious doctrines. And this makes a difference in

20

what it would mean to accept a religious doctrine. Looking ahead to some distinctions which will be developed in later chapters, these views stress a certain force which many doctrines have, namely the force of recommending courses of inward and outward action. At the same time they leave us doubtful whether any religious doctrines have (should have?) the force of proposals for belief.

Incidentally Braithwaite's and Phillips' discussions show the need for critical philosophy of religion to take serious account of the plurality of religious traditions, if we wish to keep the difference between critical philosophy of religion and theology clear. Since their main examples and references are to Christian doctrines, and since they advocate certain interpretations of Christian doctrines, such as 'God is love' (Braithwaite) and the Last Judgement (Phillips), one is tempted to suppose that they are arguing as Christian theologians. It is possible to do two things at once without serious confusion, but it is more difficult than to do one thing at a time. At any rate it makes a great deal of difference whether or not an argument should be taken in one way rather than in another, whether theological principles of judgement are being invoked or not.

Returning to our discussion of belief, certainly one can entertain something that is said, some religious doctrine for example; one may even be fascinated by it and keep it steadfastly in mind or, as Phillips puts it, the 'picture' may have a 'grip' on one; and all this without believing it in the ordinary sense. The following, like (vi), would be free from paradox:

(vii) '$p$'. It is not the case that $p$.

For example, a teacher writes the sentence $p$ on a blackboard and asks the class to consider it. Then he remarks it is untrue. Or a parent tells a fairy tale to his children at bedtime and when asked whether it really happened says 'Not really', or suggests that the question misses the point. This goes to show that ordinarily we take the first conjunct of (v) as implicitly proposing $p$ for acceptance as true, not as just reporting an inner experience or state and not as just presenting $p$ to be entertained or contemplated. That is why (v) is paradoxical.

An air of paradox would cling to the following also:

21

(viii) We believe that $p$ and teach it to our children, but there is no reason why anyone else should do so.

The reason for the air of paradox here is more complex. (a) Normally 'We believe that $p$' has the force of implicitly asserting $p$, saying that $p$ is true, as we have seen. (b) Further, asserting $p$ goes beyond presenting $p$ to be entertained by the hearer. The speaker looks for something more; he hopes his hearer will assent to $p$ or, we might say, accept his proposal that $p$ is true (or valid or right). (c) But how can he ask for assent unless he thinks there are reasons, good reasons indeed, for assent? Otherwise what could he possibly mean by assent? So it strikes us there is something logically wrong about (viii) – unless we take it as saying only that other people are free to teach their children what they believe, which in many contexts hardly needs saying. The jarring note is the implication that none of the reasons for teaching $p$ could possibly be a reason for others to do so as well. Hence condition 7 says that speakers in $S$ are ready and willing to support their proposals by giving reasons for them.

The object of this discussion of 'belief' has been to bring out what it means to put forward or propose a religious doctrine and thus to explain condition 7. But the point needs to be generalised. For it has long been recognised in the history of critical philosophy of religion that religion is not just a matter of beliefs. This was stressed in various ways by Spinoza in the 'Tractatus', by Hume in his 'Natural History of Religion', by Kant in the 'Religion', by Schleiermacher in the 'Speeches on Religion', by Rudolf Otto, and more recently by Wisdom, Hare and many others, including Braithwaite and Phillips. It would follow that proposing religious doctrines is not just a matter of proposing beliefs. Courses of inward and outward action, and valuations of experiences, objects and patterns of life are being proposed also. So the point made in condition 7 is not limited to beliefs. Its essential point as a condition of $S$ is that whatever the characters of particular doctrines held by the speakers, the speakers propose some of these doctrines for acceptance by their hearers.

The form of words employed in proposing a doctrine can vary. What makes an utterance of a doctrine a proposal of that doctrine is the force which the utterance has in the situation. Just as a

22

proposal for belief can be conveyed implicitly by an utterance of the form 'I (we) believe that $p$', so also recommendations of courses of action and proposals of valuations can be conveyed by utterances which are confessional in form.

The main point is that without proposals of doctrines the conditions for the occurrence of oppositions of doctrines would be incomplete. Suppose that all the utterances in a conversation had no other force than one or more of the following: (*a*) simple reports that some doctrine is taught in some tradition; (*b*) simple expressions of moods or inner states of a speaker; (*c*) simple declarations of a speaker's intention to act in a certain way – if these could indeed be kept simple, without any suggestion that the hearers might wish to accept the doctrines or experience the inner states or adopt the maxims of the actions. Then the existential conditions for the occurrence of oppositions of doctrines of different religions would be incomplete.

An important feature of $S$ can be brought out more clearly by developing the notion of an informative utterance and contrasting those assertions which have the force of informative utterances with those which have the force of proposals for belief. In the setting of an informative utterance it is supposed that the speaker is in a position to know what is the case whereas his hearers are not. So he can tell them what is the case. Many such utterances occur in daily life and in many special domains of inquiry. $M$ tells $N$ that he ($M$) has a pain in his back, or that he made a certain observation with a telescope, in a situation where it is supposed that $M$ is in a position to know this and that $N$ is not. On this supposition $N$, assuming $M$'s veracity, accepts what $M$ says. Then an informative utterance has occurred.

If it is not supposed that $M$ is in a position to know and that $N$ is not, an assertion is not an informative utterance. If it were supposed that both of them are in position to know, either the utterance would be pointless or it would have some emotive force or other. If it is supposed that neither is in a position to know, then the assertion becomes a step taken in a common inquiry. It has the force of a proposal for belief and reasons (other than the status of the speaker) for accepting it are in order.

In $S$ a speaker's assertions about the history of his community, its structure and activities, and what its prevailing doctrines are

23

can be informative utterances. But his assertions of doctrines do not qualify as informative utterances in $S$. For his utterances are addressed to members of other religious communities which have doctrines of their own. In the nature of the case he cannot expect them to accept the truth of his doctrines on his own authority. By virtue of the structure of the situation no one is in a position to *tell* the others what is the case when religious questions (in contrast to historical and other questions about religions) arise.

$S$ is thus different from situations where all the speakers belong to the same religious community and some speaker is in a position of religious authority, for example a bishop and his clergy, an abbot with his monks, or a teacher and his disciples. In $S$ the speakers belong to different religious communities and adhere to different traditions.

In $S$ therefore assertions which in other situations might be informative utterances are proposals for belief. In the setting of a proposal for belief the speaker may be quite sure of what he is saying and he may think he has adequate or even overwhelming grounds for certainty. Indeed condition 1 implies that he will speak from conviction. But this does not put him in a position to speak informatively, to tell the others what is the case, when he does not just report what the doctrines of his tradition are but actually asserts them. Some Hindu speaker, for example, may have immense authority in his own community so that his own disciples would be willing to accept the doctrines he teaches them on his authority. But he does not have authority here, at least not that kind of authority. Now he is speaking not to other Hindus but to Buddhists, Jews, Christians and Muslims. So his assertions of Hindu doctrines have only the force of claims which have to be developed and argued vis-à-vis competing claims.

Similarly when the utterance of a doctrine in $S$ is not an assertion but a statement of a practical doctrine, in which the speaker is putting forward a course of action to be undertaken rather than saying how things are, he is not in a position to command the course of action. This is so for two reasons. (i) In $S$ no speaker has a position of authority relative to others, so no one has a right to command. Though proposals are made seriously and maybe even urgently, no one has the required status for ordering someone else to do something. (ii) Furthermore, religious

24

courses of action involve attitudes and valuations which cannot in any case be commanded, whether in $S$ or elsewhere. Hence his utterances of practical doctrines have the force of recommending courses of action. They have to be developed and supported vis-à-vis contrasting recommendations put forward by other speakers in $S$. Both informative utterances and commands occur in situations where the speaker is in a position of authority. But this does not hold in $S$. When they advance the teachings of their religions, speakers in $S$ are no more in a position to tell others what to do than they are in a position to tell others what is the case.

Now let us notice some features of the doctrinal schemes of religions which bear on conversations in $S$. If it should turn out that some pair of doctrines of different religions proposed in $S$ are in opposition it would not follow that the doctrines of those religions are opposed at all other points. The doctrinal schemes of the major religions are not so tightly organised as all that – which is not a bad thing since it means they are capable of further development. A scheme may permit variations on some of its themes and even diverging interpretations of some of its doctrines. Still there are connections among the doctrines of a religion, some weak, some strong, and these have to be taken into account. Some doctrines depend on others. Also some doctrines are more central to a scheme than others, some more peripheral, and this will affect the importance of an opposition. The general structure of his doctrinal scheme will govern the way a speaker develops the doctrines he proposes.

One interesting and often puzzling feature of religious doctrines is the following. A doctrinal scheme may include semantic principles which say that some statements of its doctrines are symbolic while others are not, or that some are only relatively or conventionally true, while others are absolutely true. In such cases explanations of these principles would be very much in order. The hearers need to know how these semantic principles apply in order to know how the speaker means what he says. That is a practical problem which may arise in any conversation.

Now suppose a doctrinal scheme included a semantic doctrine to the following effect: While some of the doctrines of the community can be made reasonably intelligible to non-members (without guaranteeing that if understood they will be accepted),

25

others cannot. Some doctrines simply cannot be understood – not even reasonably well, by any non-members of the community. The only way in which anyone could learn to understand them at all is to become a member of the community. Then, while the speaker might exhibit this distinction between exoteric and esoteric doctrines which is built into his scheme, he could only mention the esoteric doctrines for this purpose; he could not propose them. For it would be absurd to propose something to hearers who cannot understand it.

Of course if anyone held that *no* utterance of any doctrine of his community could be intelligible, not even reasonably so, to anyone not already a member of that community, it would be against his own principle for him to participate in *S*. But none of the major religions has adopted this principle.

To make *S* plausible, all we need to assume is that the rules of speech of some religious communities permit their members, or some of them, to address proposals of some of their doctrines to members of other religious communities in appropriate circumstances, and that this is true of at least two different religions. This seems a modest assumption.

I shall not construct a flow of conversation which might occur in *S*. A number of such dialogues have been constructed for various purposes. Some like Justin Martyr's 'Dialogue with Trypho' have an apologetic purpose; some have been ways of presenting an ideal religious philosophy, like Lessing's 'Nathan the Wise'; others have been developed from an interest in the comparative study of religion and the logic of religious discourse, of which Ninian Smart's 'A Dialogue of Religions' is an excellent example. My object is only to make use of *S* as a framework for studying some types of religious utterances with a view to possible oppositions. This is a good place, however, to comment on one feature of such conversations.

It is a familiar fact about argumentative conversations that many disagreements, especially those more deeply felt, are latent not manifest. This is partly because the concepts needed to define the latent issues and make them explicit are not at hand or readily produced. This is even more likely in dialogues among speakers of different religions than in dialogues among adherents to the same tradition.

26

In the latter case a large supply of common concepts is available. Furthermore, the speakers can rely on a common store of incompletely conceptualised experience, which can yield new concepts when they are needed to make issues explicit. This is less true of situations like $S$, where there is a smaller supply of common concepts and where speakers have a narrower range of concrete religious experiences and activities in common.

Hence in situations like $S$ much lies below the level of what the speakers say. An analogy may suggest the point. Contacts of physical objects occur at particular points on their surfaces, but the force vectors are determined by subsurface masses and structures. Something like this is true of many conversations and is especially true of conversations among adherents to different religious traditions. It is also true that sometimes speakers find ways to bring these latent disagreements into the open, to put obscurely felt oppositions into words.

# 3  A Problematical Case

In a situation approximating $S$ the conversation is likely to gravitate towards the central doctrines of the religions, though it may verge on them gradually and circuitously by way of peripheral questions. Speakers may have to feel their way along as they try to find out how other speakers formulate the central doctrines of their religions and what these formulas imply. It may take time and patience to understand the central issues at stake.

A doctrine is central in some scheme to the degree that other doctrines are either derivable from it or depend on it. Often its centrality is reflected by its importance in creeds, manuals of instruction and discipline, and guides for meditation or worship. But this may not be so. Many important doctrines are taken for granted; the community has not been spurred by historical circumstances to formulate and develop them. The central doctrines of a religion are not always those most disputed with outsiders.

We can make a few generalisations, mainly negative, about the central doctrines of the major religions. Historical claims are important in some religious traditions, but ordinarily their central doctrines are not strictly historical claims. A strictly historical claim is one which can be settled, so far as it can be settled, by historical methods, including archaeology, documentary criticism, and so on. It is a claim that some event or nexus of events, under some description, did or did not actually occur.

Some of the major religions have doctrines which claim that certain historical events occurred, for example: that Moses led the Israelites through the wilderness of Sinai; that Gautama left his home and took up an ascetic life, that he sat in meditation under a pipul tree and afterwards taught certain doctrines; that

28

Jesus of Nazareth suffered under Pontius Pilate, was crucified, dead, and buried; that Muhammad recited the verses which constitute the Qur'ān; and many others.

It is striking that historical counter-claims occur only rarely in doctrines of the major religions. Of course it is not uncommon for an historical claim to be denied by outsiders. It is decidedly uncommon, however, to find, as a doctrine of some religion, a claim that some event *e* did in fact occur and, as a doctrine of some other religion, a claim that *e* did not in fact occur. The clearest case of this sort I have found is the denial of the Christian claim that Jesus was crucified, in Sura 4 (verse 156) of the Qur'ān: 'they did not slay him, neither crucified him, only a likeness of that was shown to them' (1).

There are various reasons why such historical counter-claims are seldom embodied in doctrinal schemes. Some religions are less historically oriented than others; some are relatively unconcerned with particular historical events. Also, some pairs of religions arose in very different historical environments. Even so the rarity of these oppositions is striking and suggestive.

Oppositions of strictly historical claims between religions would be relatively unproblematical, not because they could be settled easily but because it is clear how they would have to be settled, namely by historical analysis and investigation.

Though strictly historical claims are essential to some of the central doctrines of some religions, none of these central doctrines is itself just an historical claim. It is a central doctrine of Buddhism that Gautama attained enlightenment, and it is a central doctrine of Christianity that Jesus Christ died to save mankind, and it is a central doctrine of Islam that Allah spoke the words of the Qur'ān to Muhammad. These doctrines would not follow from the historical claims alone. They involve interpretations of the historical events and valuations of knowing them.

Oppositions involving interpretations of particular historical events (speculative interpretations, for example) and valuations of knowing particular historical truths would be much more complex and more problematical than oppositions of strictly historical claims. At the same time they would reflect more clearly the range of problems with which the doctrines of the major religions

29

deal. This would be true also of doctrines about the significance and importance of historical events generally, where oppositions (e.g., between Hindu and Christian doctrines) might well be found.

Similarly the central doctrines of the major traditions are not scientific theories, that is to say exact formulations of uniformities said to hold in the apparent world, or explanations and predictions derived from these laws of nature. This is still true even when the concept of a religion is extended to cover versions of 'the religion of science' (2). For in these cases the central doctrines are not themselves scientific theories but instead doctrines about the place of man in the universe. Sometimes in versions of 'the religion of science' it seems to be argued that these latter doctrines are dependent on, or even sometimes (implausibly) that they can be deduced from, scientific theories. But even if this were so it would not turn the scientific theories themselves into religious doctrines. Instead, what would be claimed is that certain religious doctrines depend on or follow from scientific truths.

Though conceivably a religious tradition might include among its subsidiary doctrines some scientific claim (or something purporting to be a scientific claim), oppositions of such doctrines drawn from different religions are even less likely than opposed historical claims, and for analogous reasons. Additional reasons are that (i) all the major religions took shape in pre-scientific eras and (ii) when they have had to assimilate modern science they have learned (more or less, sometimes by bitter experience) how to avoid introducing scientific theories into their doctrinal schemes. But as with historical claims the main reason is that religious doctrines deal with a different range of problems than scientific theories do, and that a religion which loses a clear sense of the problems to which its doctrines are addressed is unlikely to survive.

More important and more problematical oppositions occur among religious interpretations of scientific truths and valuations of knowing them. But these interpretations and valuations depend on doctrines which are more central to the respective doctrinal schemes (3).

It is much more difficult to plot connections of religious doctrines with moral claims and speculative claims. Generally speaking we are less clear about what these claims are and how they

30

might be settled, than about historical and scientific claims. It would be agreed generally that though all the major religions teach moral standards and rules their central doctrines are not identical with these, and that, though some religions include speculative claims in their doctrinal schemes, their central doctrines are not identical with these. Usually in the major religions both moral doctrines and speculative doctrines are bound up in intimate and complicated ways with distinctively religious valuations, and the distinctions and connections among these are not always easy to fathom. We can get some light on this later on.

As a generalisation it seems fair to say that the major religions all present and teach patterns of life. This is not absolutely distinctive of religious systems, since there are also patterns of life we would not call religious (4). But it is characteristic of the major religions, and this can furnish a perspective on what speakers in S are doing. As a speaker goes on explaining and supporting doctrines of his religion it would become evident that the doctrines are connected with one another, and that in putting forward these doctrines he is making an overall recommendation of a pattern of life.

In some doctrines he is recommending courses of action, inward or outward. In other doctrines he is proposing that various experiences, existents and conditions of existence be valued in certain ways. In other doctrines he is proposing beliefs about how things are. Many utterances of doctrines will have more than one of these functions. And the overall point of these utterances as a whole is to advance a certain pattern of life. The courses of action, the valuations and the beliefs are ingredients in this pattern.

Sometimes when we listen to proponents of different religions it seems fairly clear at the outset that they are disagreeing with one another. Consider the following pairs of doctrines:

Salvation comes through faith in Amida's Original Vow.
Salvation comes through faith in Jesus Christ.

The self is eternal.
There is no unchanging self; all things are impermanent.

Each man has only one life to live.
There are many rebirths.

31

Freedom consists in realisation of unity with Brahman.
Freedom consists in serving God.

An arhat is greater than all the gods.
God is the maker and Lord of all men.

Ignorance is the root of evil.
Sin is the root of evil.

In these cases we are likely to have a strong impression that the doctrines are in opposition to one another, even though later on we may have second and less confident thoughts about this.

Other cases are more problematical. In these problematical cases, on one hand we suspect that an opposition lurks behind the formulations. We may suspect this from acquaintance with their historical contexts, or from the way their proponents speak – they speak as though an issue is at stake – or from their logical forms. On the other hand no explicit opposition is apparent. If we pay attention only to the formulations themselves it seems as though two thoughts are being launched like ships with different destinations and whose paths do not cross. So we are puzzled. Could the doctrines be accepted jointly without absurdity, or not?

I shall develop a case of this latter sort, a contrast of doctrines which exhibits no explicit oppositions, because a problematical case can teach us more about our subject than an easier case could. It will be obvious that the sentences I use in developing the case are suggested to me by Buddhist literature and by the literature of Judaism. But I do not wish to claim that I am correctly stating Buddhist doctrines or Judaic doctrines, for reasons I have already explained. So this should be taken as a hypothetical case, which would be sufficient to show some of the ways in which oppositions of doctrines of different religions are possible.

It would be unfortunate if readers should expect to learn much about Buddhism or Judaism from this essay. I am not a historian, and on the other hand I am not in a position to speak for either tradition. I wish to deal with a philosophical problem, and my choices of sentences are guided by a requirement of the problem, the need to bring out symmetries and asymmetries of different doctrinal schemes. It could be objected that these formulas are

32

misleading because (i) they are only skeletons of doctrines (how could a doctrine be compressed into a single short sentence?) or because (ii) they represent certain strands of the schemes and not others. But let us suppose that speakers in $S$ would amplify them and that other strands would be introduced into the conversation as it proceeded. All that is needed for our purpose is this supposition: that well-educated speakers in $S$ might say these things *among others* at some point or other in the conversation.

Probably it will be evident that Buddhist ways of thinking are stranger to me than Judaic ways of thinking, and I assume this will be true of most readers. That is why there is more explication of B-formulas than of J-formulas. At the same time it must be said that Christians are likely to assume they understand Judaism much better than they actually do, so allowance must be made for that too.

By limiting ourselves to this one case we shall fail to cover many points which would come up if we should study contrasts suggested by the literatures of Hinduism and Islam, or of Buddhism and Christianity, or of other pairs of religions. Still it may be better to study one case in depth than to cover more ground in a short essay.

Let us begin with the following pair of sentences:

B1   The Dharma is the path to attainment of Nirvana.
J1   The Torah teaches us to respond rightly to God.

In B1 'the Dharma' denotes the teachings of the Buddha, though 'dharma' has other meanings in other contexts. In this sense it figures in the primary act of veneration, resolution and training, namely:

I take refuge in the Buddha.
I take refuge in the Dharma.
I take refuge in the Sangha.

The literature also speaks of the Dharma as a raft which carries one across the waters of conditioned existence, where nothing is permanent, to the farther shore of Nirvana, the matchless state of security and peace. In J1 'the Torah' denotes the teachings of the Bible, which Christians refer to as the Old Testament, as

33

interpreted in the tradition. Love, obedience and service are said to be due to God.

Now suppose that B1 is uttered in $S$ and that J1 is uttered in response. Then we ask, Does this response constitute a disagreement? Are B1 and J1 not just in contrast but in opposition to one another? No opposition lies on the surface of the sentences. J1 does not say the Torah is the path, or even a path to Nirvana. B1 does not say that the Dharma teaches responses to God. Neither speaks of responding to Nirvana nor of attaining God. 'The Dharma' and 'the Torah' have different referents, and let us suppose that 'Nirvana' and 'God' have different referents also. Then there is no obvious point at which the sentences give a foothold for an opposition.

In spite of this absence of explicit oppositions it does not seem plausible that anyone could accept both of these doctrines, that is to say, be ready and willing to assert both of them and to act on their practical implications, without involving himself in an absurdity of some kind. But if so (the reader's initial intuition about that may be different from my own) the opposition must lie below the surface and could be made explicit only by connecting utterances of these sentences with other possible utterances which they involve in some way, and seeing whether some of these other utterances would be in opposition.

That is the procedure we follow in many ordinary cases. We are puzzled about what a speaker has said because we are not sure what his consistency-rules are. We discover what they are by asking whether this or that implication holds or not. Likewise the doctrines of a religion have their own consistency-rules, their own way of hanging together in a scheme.

Sometimes this is thought to be a peculiarity of religious discourse. For example, Austin Farrer construes schemes of religious doctrines as sets of 'parables' and says:

> The art of balancing parables is acquired in use by believers, without their being conscious of it. That they use such an art becomes evident as soon as we attempt to fix upon them all the apparent logical consequences from any single parable. They will then begin to pick and choose, admitting some consequences and refusing others; and if we ask them why, they

34

will draw in further parables supporting what they allow, and hostile to what they reject (5).

But if we discount the dubious suggestion that all religious doctrines are parables (imaginative narratives?) this makes quite a general point and makes it very well. It implies that speakers do have rules for admitting or rejecting consequences, even if they cannot fomulate all of them. If the picking and choosing were purely arbitrary, speakers would forfeit any claim to serious consideration of what they say.

Just as I shall not attempt historical justifications of the formulas in the B-series and in the J-series, I shall not do so for the connections among them, and for the same reason. For our purpose a hypothetical case is sufficient.

So I shall show how B1 might be connected with the following:

B2   Aim at attaining Nirvana.
B3   Live in accord with the Dharma.
B4   Attainment of Nirvana is the only possible way of emancipation from suffering, which is intrinsic to conditioned existence.

And from this it should be clear how J1 might be connected with:

J2   Respond rightly to God.
J3   Live in accord with the Torah.
J4   God is our Lord and Maker, creator of heaven and earth and all that is in them, the judge of all nations and the fountain of life.

This will also indicate how the doctrines of a religion can be connected in a doctrinal scheme. Then beginning in the next chapter we can develop some possible oppositions between members of the B-series and members of the J-series.

The connection between B1 and B2 can be approached by considering:

B1′   If you want to attain Nirvana, live in accord with the Dharma.

Now B1′ follows from B1 in $S$. That is to say, if a speaker utters

35

B1 in $S$ and then refuses (not just fails) to utter B1' without a good excuse, he is acting inconsistently. Among good excuses for refusing to say something at some point or other in the conversation would be for example: (i) the hearer already knows it; (ii) the speaker wishes to allow the hearer to reach the conclusion himself; (iii) the hearer will attach unwanted meanings to the sentence. Analogously an utterance in 1968 of:

K    The Kline Biology Tower is the tallest building in New Haven

would require, in the above sense, an utterance of:

K'    If you want to see the tallest building in New Haven, look at the Kline Biology Tower.

Both the speaker of B1 and the speaker of K should be ready and willing to address the corresponding sentences and if either refuses to do so in appropriate circumstances he is acting inconsistently.

But B1', though it follows from B1, is not equivalent to B1. An utterance of B1 in $S$ says more than B1' does, and B2 (Aim at attaining Nirvana) formulates part of this surplus meaning of B1. This can be seen in the following way. B1' by itself is like a case where someone on the wayside, say a highway patrolman at a cross-roads, gives directions for going to Boston ('If you want to go to Boston keep straight ahead'), but would be equally ready and willing to direct the traveller to New York. It is indifferent to him which way the traveller wants to go. But it cannot be that all utterances of the sentence B1 in $S$ have this neutral informative force.

It is true that the sentence B1 might occur in $S$ as an elliptical version of 'In Buddhist teaching, the Dharma is the path to Nirvana', and might in this case have only informative force. But it cannot occur only in this way. For one condition of $S$ is that speakers express their convictions and propose their doctrines. $S$ is thus unlike a meeting of scholars to exchange information about the teachings of various religions. Another condition is that the participants are reasonably well informed, minimising the need for information of this sort.

When an utterance of B1 in $S$ expresses a conviction and makes

36

a proposal, the speaker is not equally ready and willing to make an alternative conditional recommendation, for example 'If you want to be saved from sin, believe in Christ'. So he is in a very different position from the patrolman at the cross-roads. In uttering B1 he is implicitly recommending that the hearer should aim at attaining Nirvana. In this way the utterance of B1 is stronger than the conditional recommendation B1'; it implies the unconditional recommendation B2: Aim at attaining Nirvana.

So the utterance of B1 in S commits the speaker to being ready and willing to utter B2 on the right occasion. If someone should take B1 as equivalent to B1' he would miss the point. Suppose someone unsure of the point of B1 should respond with 'And you are recommending that we aim at attaining Nirvana?' The speaker of B1 might remain silent, perhaps for pedagogical reasons. He might think this is not quite the right occasion (or, of course, be puzzled why the point is not already clear). But if in the circumstances he should disown B2 he would be acting inconsistently. Similarly J2 (Respond rightly to God) follows from J1.

Coming now to B3 (Live according to the Dharma), it seems clear that this follows from B1' taken together with B2, and hence follows from B1 in the sense explained above. If anyone makes the conditional recommendation B1' (which the utterance of B1 requires) and the unconditional recommendation B2 (which B1 requires also) and then refuses to make the unconditional recommendation B3, he is acting inconsistently. Similarly J3 follows from J1' and J2 taken together, and hence from J1.

The only escape route would be a plea that B1' leaves the speaker free to recommend other paths to attainment of Nirvana. This loophole is easily plugged by attention to the second definite article in B1 (*the* path), of which a strong interpretation is certainly required for historical plausibility, with a consequent strengthening of B1' (If you want to attain Nirvana, the only way to do so is to live in accord with the Dharma).

It would have been possible to reverse the order in which B2 and B3 have been reached. B2 would follow from B3 and B1 taken together. The Dharma itself directs life to attaining Nirvana. The Dharma does not, like a cooking recipe, present a rule for attaining an optional end, which is itself left as a matter of indifference. It is not a map of various patterns of life; it presents the discipline of a particular pattern of life in which attaining Nirvana is central. It so construes the general conditions of human existence and the experience of Gautama in particular as to incite an aim at attaining Nirvana, to arouse hope of attainment, and to give reasons for directing life in this way. So a recommendation to live according to the Dharma implies a recommendation to aim at attaining Nirvana. One cannot live in accord with the Dharma without, sooner or later, aiming at attaining Nirvana.

Similarly J2 would follow from J3 and J1 taken together. The Torah not only explains how to respond rightly to God, as though this were in itself an unstructured ideal; it lays down a pattern of life in which rightly responding to God is the central structural element. It construes the general conditions of life and in particular the history of Israel in such a way as to awaken right responses to God and to give reasons for adopting the pattern of life in which these are central.

Further, we could have reached B3 from B1, and J3 from J1, directly by way of condition 7 of *S*. If the force of B1 and J1 is such that B2 and J2 are unconditional recommendations, it would be equally true that B3 and J3 are unconditional recommendations. It is not necessary, for an unconditional recommendation, that a speaker should require of the hearer a conscious aim at the outcome of the course of action which is being recommended. It is possible to begin to live in a certain way and then to *find* what the outcome or the point of the process is; one finds oneself on the path to Nirvana or in a certain relation to God. This is true of how any pattern of life is acquired.

That needs to be said especially about B2 though it applies to J2 also. The literature speaks of aiming at Nirvana as a goal but it explains this can be misleading since (i) a craving for Nirvana is a hindrance – craving must be got rid of in principle; and (ii) Nirvana cannot be attained by crafty techniques and devices. Straining to attain Nirvana, or to respond rightly to God, can be self-defeating.

An unconditional recommendation is not a command. A speaker can unconditionally recommend some course of action which he is not in a position to command. Nor is it something for

38

which no reason need be given, i.e. an arbitrary recommendation. Indeed, as we shall see later, the notion of an arbitrary recommendation would involve an absurdity. There can be arbitrary commands but not arbitrary recommendations.

B4 (Attainment of Nirvana is the only possible way of emancipation from suffering, which is intrinsic to conditioned existence) and J4 (God is our Lord and Maker, the creator of heaven and earth and all that is in them, the judge of all nations and the fountain of life) are not as tightly linked to B1 and J1 as B2–3 and J2–3 are. They are representative of a number of utterances which are likely to occur in $S$; B1 and J1 call for some utterances or other of this kind.

An utterance of B4 is different from B2 and B3. Though it would have seemed unnatural and inappropriate to respond to B2 or B3 by saying 'That is true' or 'That is untrue', these appraisals seem natural and appropriate to B4. It proposes something, but what it puts forward is not an aim for the hearer to adopt or a course of action to be undertaken but instead an account of the way things are. It is a proposal for belief. How is it connected with B1, B2 and B3?

One of its functions is to help explain the concept of attaining Nirvana. Thus B1 depends on B4 (and on other explanations) for its meaning. So also J4 helps to explain the concept of God. But explaining concepts cannot be the whole function of an utterance of B4 in $S$. That could be done without asserting B4, by putting quotation marks around the sentence as it were, giving it the force of 'When Buddhists speak of Nirvana what they mean is . . .'. But, under condition 7, B4 is asserted and one function of the assertion is to give in short compass a reason for adoption of the recommendation B2. The point is not just to explain the sense of 'Nirvana'; it gives a reason for aiming at attaining Nirvana. It asserts something about the conditions of human life in view of which it is reasonable to do this. Similarly the assertion of J4 gives a complex reason for adopting a different pattern of life. Thus in both cases the speakers are not acting arbitrarily in making their recommendations. Each is making a set of recommendations in view of the conditions of life as he understands them. He is ready and willing to support the recommendation B2 as condition 7 requires.

B4 gives a reason for adopting B2, but an assertion of B4 in $S$ does not terminate inquiry and argument. No speaker in $S$ is in a position to be informative on such matters any more than he is in a position to command courses of action. Hence objections to B4 and J4 are in order and call for replies. The situation is open for anyone to argue against B4, for example, (i) that suffering is not intrinsic to conditioned existence, or (ii) that there are other ways of emancipation from suffering, or (iii) that in aiming at Nirvana one pays too great a price for emancipation from suffering. Comparable objections to J4 are also in order, and some of them are familiar to us all.

The connection of B4 with B3 is an interesting one. B4 is a summary of some of the teachings of the Dharma, in particular of the Four Noble Truths. So also J4 summarises some of the teachings of the Torah. Now ordinarily, when a speaker recommends living in accord with some body of teachings which includes statements as well as rules of action, we think he is seriously proposing that the statements included in the teachings are true. We suppose that he himself thinks they are true, and that he is proposing to his hearers that they are true. He believes them, and he puts them forward with a view to his hearers believing them. He sees the world in a certain way and he is ready and willing to give an account of the way things are as he sees them.

So these beliefs are ingredients in the pattern of life which is being recommended. Believing that certain conditions of existence hold and that the possibilities of life depend on these conditions is part of what it means to live in accord with the Dharma or to live in accord wth the Torah. Ordinarily we suppose the major religions view their teachings in this way, and on the whole this supposition seems valid.

Now suppose that someone who recommends living in accord with some body of teachings should give a different account of what he is doing. He says that living in accord with the teachings implies undertaking the courses of action set forth in the teachings, but it does not imply believing the statements included in the teachings; it only implies entertaining them. The sentences used in the statements are to be held in mind and contemplated. This is all that is required and nothing further about these statements is being claimed. The speaker does not believe or disbelieve them. He does not claim they are true, and he does not object to someone's saying they are untrue, except perhaps by pointing out that 'true' and 'untrue' do not properly apply to them.

He may think that entertaining the statements has some intrinsic value, as when we read and enjoy poetry without believing or disbelieving what is said. Or he may think it will have some causal influence on our attitudes and actions. Braithwaite takes this view. Or he may take the view that reflecting on the sentences in certain ways will lead to experiences of 'disclosure', as Ian T. Ramsey does. (6)

In respect of what it leaves out, this explanation varies from the way major religions generally explain their teachings. I shall assume that speakers in S are likely to intend B4 and J4 (and comparable utterances) as assertions in a stronger sense, but it would not be right to rule out this other kind of explanation. Speakers in S have to be responsible to the principles of their own traditions.

Our business at the moment is to see how this would affect the connections of B4 and J4 with B2–3 and J2–3 and hence with B1 and J1. It would seem to give B4 and J4 the force of recommendations of (inward) courses of action instead of the force of assertions. An explicit expression of the force this explanation would give them would be: Entertain (imagine? contemplate? reflect on?) '. . .' where the sentences B4 or J4 are substituted for the dots inside the quotation marks (7).

Now if B4 is a course-of-action recommendation it cannot function as a reason in support of other course-of-action recommendations. So uttering B4 would not be giving a reason for accepting B2 or B3. Perhaps it would be recommending a procedure that is involved in undertaking what B2 and B3 recommend. But if B4 and comparable utterances do not give reasons for accepting the speaker's course-of-action recommendations, how could such reasons be given?

Someone can command a course of action without giving reasons for undertaking it (8), other than threats and promises. But B2 and B3 cannot be commands in S, or anywhere else for that matter. They can have no stronger force than that of recommendations. Now recommendations cannot be arbitrary in the

41

way commands can. A course of action is recommended *as* possible and desirable or right (perhaps even as morally necessary) under the circumstances. So reasons for undertaking the course of action are called for and objections to doing so are in order. Then it seems that on this explanation of B4, though reasons for undertaking courses of action are called for, none can be given.

Finally we can sum up the structure of the problematical case as follows: An utterance of B1 in $S$ commits the speaker to being ready and willing to utter B2, B3 and B4 (or some comparable assertion) on appropriate occasions, and the same is true of the J-series. If he should refuse to so do on such occasions he would be acting inconsistently. He would lay himself open to the charge that he was not being serious in uttering B1, or to the charge that he did not realise what he was doing.

His saying that the Dharma is the path to Nirvana conveys implicitly a recommendation to aim at attaining Nirvana and an accompanying recommendation to live in accord with the Dharma. He is further committed to explain what is meant by Nirvana and the Dharma and to give reasons in support of his recommendations.

Thus he is in effect presenting a pattern of life, which includes an aim, courses of action, and beliefs. The speaker of J1 presents a different pattern of life, with a different centre of meaning, different courses of action, and different beliefs. Later on we will pay special attention to the valuations which are built into religious patterns of life, and their connections with courses of action and beliefs.

Now we are in a better position to ask how the utterances of B1 and J1 in $S$ are opposed, if indeed they are. For they are opposed if some pair of utterances required by them are opposed.

# 4 Recommendations of Courses of Action

Most of this chapter is about oppositions of those religious doctrines which recommend specific courses of action, but first we should develop the background for this a little further. The point of the B-series of utterances as a whole is to recommend a certain pattern of life; the point of the J-series is to recommend a different pattern. Let us ask a question whose force is logical rather than historical, the hypothetical question: How could these overall recommendations be opposed?

The initial answer is that they are opposed if the recommended patterns of life are incompatible for joint realisation. Two patterns are incompatible for some individual if it is impossible (logically, or because of laws of nature, or because of his own constitution, or practically) for him to realise both patterns together, to live in accord with both patterns. And two patterns are incompatible without restriction if no one can realise both of them together. For example, it was impossible for James Thurber's Walter Mitty to live his ordinary life and also be a resourceful ship's captain braving terrible storms at sea; hence his 'secret life' in fantasy. Again, Kierkegaard seems to argue in 'Either/ Or' that it is impossible for anyone to be both a Johannes (of 'The Diary of a Seducer') and a Judge William. So if the pattern of life recommended in the B-series and that in the J-series cannot both be realised in the life of someone, and if both recommendations are addressed to that person, then these recommendations are in opposition. And if the patterns of life cannot be realised together by anyone, then the doctrines are in opposition in all cases.

This initial answer is not very helpful unless we go further and take account of the complexity of a pattern of life and the corresponding complexity of the utterances involved in recommending it, in our case the complexity of religious doctrines. We can do this in the following way.

Two patterns of life are incompatible if some pair of their ingredients (courses of action, valuations, beliefs) are incompatible, that is to say: (i) if some pair of courses of action cannot both be carried out and hence cannot be undertaken without absurdity; or (ii) if some pair of valuations cannot be made jointly without absurdity; or (iii) if some pair of propositions cannot both be true and hence cannot be believed or asserted without absurdity; or (iv) if some pair of heterogeneous ingredients cannot both be realised, for example if it is impossible without absurdity both to undertake some course of action belonging to one pattern and to hold some belief which belongs to the other.

It follows that two recommendations of patterns of life are opposed if some pair of utterances involved in the recommendations are opposed, that is to say if (i) some pair of recommendations of courses of action or (ii) some pair of proposals of valuations or (iii) some pair of proposals for belief or (iv) some pair of heterogeneous utterances cannot both be accepted without absurdity.

Now, to study how doctrines recommending courses of action can be opposed, let us develop our problematical case further. From B2 (Aim at attaining Nirvana) we can derive

B2.1   Direct life to Nirvana

and from J2 (Respond rightly to God) we can derive

J2.1   Direct life to God.

Anyone who utters B2 or J2 seriously and knowing what he is doing would be ready and willing to say at least as much as B2.1 or J2.1; he would wish to say a great deal more also.

In particular he would wish to say more about the manner of directing life he is recommending. For the manner of directing life must befit that to which life is directed, and here B2 and J2 differ in a striking way. In B2 the manner of directing life consists in aiming at attainment of a certain state. In J2 the manner of directing life consists in responding to a present reality. So B2.1 and J2.1 do not exhaust the meanings of B2 and J2, and consideration of the difference between these manners of direct-

44

ing life would open up a deeper dimension of contrast between them. For the time being let us consider only B2.1 and J2.1.

Let us take it that B2.1 does not restrict interests to Nirvana by excluding genuine and intense interests in other states or things, and that J2.1 does not restrict interests to God alone. This is plausible since religious patterns of life generally make room for and often encourage a multiplicity of interests and activities. Thus, let us say, many other aims and responses are compatible with directing life to Nirvana or to God, and may be permitted or even required by B2.1 or J2.1, for example artistic or scientific projects, carrying out one's duties as a monk or as a parent or as a citizen, being affectionate and responsible to other people, enjoying natural objects and works of art, promoting the welfare of Sangha or of the people of Israel, and so on. Let us suppose that directing life to Nirvana does not require directing all of one's interests and practical intentions to Nirvana only, and that directing life to God does not require directing all one's interests and practical intentions to God only.

It is true that sometimes we encounter religious utterances which seem to imply something of the form: Have no other interest than an interest in ———. Often we are justified in taking the language as hyperbolic. If taken strictly and seriously these utterances would suggest an abnormal and obsessive form of life, to which William James's comments on the 'excesses of saintliness' would apply:

In the life of saints, technically so called, the spiritual faculties are strong, but what gives the impression of extravagance proves usually on examination to be a relative deficiency of intellect. Spiritual excitement takes pathological forms whenever other interests are too few and the intellect too narrow (1)

Though religious devotion does sometimes take an exclusivist form the major religions all encourage or at least permit a variety of interests and activities. If their teachings were utterly exclusivist (otherworldly), they could hardly have survived as institutions. So we should leave the way open for non-exclusivist interpretations of B2.1 and J2.1.

On the other hand the patterns of life presented by the major

45

religions all focus life in some way and give it some direction. So it is not as though the speakers were saying just 'I recommend that, among other things, you . . .'. These are not just *inter alia* recommendations. Though the major religions make room for a number of interests and practical intentions, their patterns of life relate these to some central direction. For this reason we hesitate to call some interest or activity religious if it is directed to something taken just as one of a number of things.

So, to do justice to both these features of the major religions, namely that they admit a multiplicity of human interests and that they relate these to something valued in a distinctive way, we ought to amplify B2.1 and J2.1 by adding to 'direct life' some such adverbial qualifier as 'as a whole' or 'on the whole' or 'above all'. The differences among these qualifiers might themselves suggest different manners of patterning life but we can leave these differences to one side and take them as roughly interchangeable. Thus we arrive at:

B2.2   Direct life as a whole to Nirvana.
J2.2   Direct life as a whole to God.

These recommendations summarise comprehensive policies for living. They indicate general courses of action and can yield maxims such as:

I shall direct the course of my life as a whole so as to attain Nirvana.
I shall direct the course of my life as a whole so as to respond rightly to God.

Now B2.2 and J2.2 seem to formulate an explicit opposition since they seem to recommend incompatible courses of action. But this depends on a point which can be brought out by recasting these recommendations awkwardly as quasi-assertions:

B2.3   Nirvana is that to which life as a whole should be directed.
J2.3   God is that to which life as a whole should be directed.

By virtue of the qualifier 'as a whole' (or 'on the whole' or 'above all') the predicate common to B2.3 and J2.3 is a uniquely-applying predicate; a speaker cannot assert it of two or more

46

logical subjects without inconsistency. So these utterances are in opposition unless the speakers are referring to one and the same logical subject under different names, which might be more plausible of the following pair:

Allah is that to which life as a whole should be directed.
God is that to which life as a whole should be directed.

For no one is likely to say that both 'God' and 'Allah' refer successfully unless they refer to the same being. Both Muslims and Jews are monotheists. But this escape route from opposition does not seem feasible in B2.2 and J2.2. To say the least, much tortuous doctrinal development would be required to show that the references to Nirvana and to God converge to one and the same referent. Still, we need only the hypothetical point that if different logical subjects are being referred to, then what is said in one of them is opposed to what is said in the other.

Thus the opposition of B2.3 and J2.3 depends on two conditions: (i) that because of the 'as a whole' qualifier the predicate cannot be applied consistently to both of two logical subjects, and (ii) that the logical subjects of the quasi-assertions are not identical. The first point is syntactical; the second point is semantic and assumes that the uses of 'Nirvana' and 'God' are governed by traditions and that they have different referents. Any tradition undergoes development, and if the traditions were so developed that the references converged to an identity then this particular opposition would evaporate.

Now let us reflect on the different manners of directing life that are being recommended, so as to bring out another and perhaps an even deeper difference between B2 and J2 than is reflected in B2.2 and J2.2. This further difference is unlike the difference between:

The main aim and end of life is to attain Nirvana.
The main aim and end of life is to attain the vision of God.

For both of these, we might say, express teleological conceptions of life. Each orients life to an end, though to a different end. But J2 suggests a different manner of orientation, not to an end but to a reality, a non-teleological orientation. Life is centred not on an end to be attained but on a reality to be responded to. For

47

the sake of the argument let us imagine a speaker of J2 saying: The main point of life is not to attain some end. We shouldn't organise our lives as wholes around some end we aim to attain. We should organise them in a different manner. What matters most is to respond rightly, that is to say appropriately, appreciatively and fully, to something which is at least as real and present as we are.

The proponent of B2 does not thereby deny that there are real things to be responded to in the course of life, and the proponent of J2 does not thereby deny there are aims to be attained. We should not take an implausible case where one speaker has no room in his conception of life for responsibility, in the strong and complex sense developed by H. Richard Niebuhr in 'The Responsible Self' (2), and the other has no room for teleology. The point is that in his conception of life as a whole the speaker of B2 subordinates responsibility to teleology; with J2 it is the other way around.

It is an interesting but difficult question whether this difference necessarily involves an opposition. I shall not pursue this question, since the upshot would not affect the fact that B2.2 and J2.2 are opposed in the way brought out by B2.3 and J2.3.

That is not the only way B2.2 and J2.2 can be opposed. Suppose we construe them as recommending comprehensive courses of action, courses of action which range over the whole of a lifespan and apply to all the activity involved in a life. Then B2.2 and J2.2 present practical ways of life and not just orientations to life (3). A practical way of life involves something more than a set of attitudes, of valuations and beliefs; it involves some specific courses of action which contribute to the shaping of inward and outward life as a whole. Then undertaking to direct life to Nirvana, or to God, would involve undertaking certain specific courses of action and not others. So the utterances might be opposed in a different way than in their orientations to life as brought out by B2.3 and J2.3. They would be opposed if some of the specific courses of action they involve are incompatible with one another.

The major religions do indeed teach practical ways of life in which comprehensive courses of action are tied to specific courses of action. As a generalisation this seems fair and just, but it is

48

only a generalisation and not a rule. Any religious tradition has the option to develop its doctrines in such a way that this would not be true of it. Its teachers are free, from external constraint at least, to claim that the tradition does not tie its pattern of life, by way of rules and principles, to any specific courses of action whatever. As a consequence its pattern of life would consist in a set of valuations and beliefs; it would not be a practical way of life in the above sense.

Whether this is true of some religion as a matter of fact is an historical or phenomenological question. It is worth noting as a matter of historical interest that often antinomian movements differ from their traditions not by detaching their way of life from all specific courses of action whatever but instead by re-defining the specific actions which that way of life requires. Specific rules for meditation or spiritual exercises or worship may be substituted for moral rules, for example.

Whether on the other hand some religion should, to be true to its tradition, develop its doctrines in this way, is a question for its own teachers to determine, not a question for philosophers of religion. Critical philosophy of religion cannot substitute for a religion's development of its own doctrines, nor the other way around. Both enterprises will suffer if either fails to accept its own limits and do its own work.

In the B-series and in the J-series, general rules for specifying courses of action occur in B3 (Live in accord with the Dharma) and J3 (Live in accord with the Torah). Suppose that these bodies of teachings, the Dharma and the Torah, are not collections of miscellaneous and unrelated facts and rules, however unsystematically their parts may be arranged; suppose that in each case the teachings adumbrate a pattern which gives life an overall meaning and direction. Suppose also that each includes doctrines which recommend specific courses of action. Then accepting B3 or J3 would require something more than having a set of valuations and beliefs; it would require also undertaking specific courses of action. Consider in connection with B3 the following specific courses of action (4):

building a temple
becoming a monk and keeping the monastic rules (vinaya)

49

giving alms to monks

placing flowers or burning incense before a Buddha image

refraining from taking life

And consider in connection with J3 the following:

keeping the Sabbath

participating in festivals and holy days

observing dietary laws, which give bodily functions religious
import

contributing to Jews in distress

supporting oppressed people

Both these lists could be revised by omissions, additions and
reformulations. Now *B* might or might not wish to say of any
course of action on the first list, however it should be revised,
that that course of action is absolutely essential to the comprehensive course of action he recommends. And *J* might or might
not wish to say this of any course of action on the second list. But
*B* might well wish to say that accepting B3 does require undertaking some courses of action on the revised list, so that if someone says he accepts B3 but undertakes none of them then he has
not understood B3 or else he is not in earnest. And *J* might well
say something similar of J3.

A number of these courses of action are ways of participating
in the life of a particular community; they involve institutional
actions. All the major religions teach doctrines which have this
effect – and all the minor ones too for that matter, if they are at
all well developed, for we hesitate to speak of something as
'a religion' if it involves no concept at all of a particular community. According to the Dharma the primary ritual act is
'taking the three refuges' which includes 'I take refuge in the
Sangha.' The Sangha, the order of monks and nuns, is the core of
the Buddhist community and laymen have obligations to support
it and promote its welfare. Likewise many teachings of the
Torah have the effect of strengthening the people Israel and
maintaining its existence. These facts give support to a common
assumption; ordinarily we would be rightly puzzled if someone
claimed to be a Buddhist or a Jew and if none of his actions
identified him with any Buddhist or Jewish institutions.

50

Now consider some specific courses of action of a somewhat different sort and on a different scale. These are, for B3, the discipline of meditation and for J3 studying the Torah.

The discipline of meditation is part of a threefold discipline which is in turn both a condensation and a development of the Noble Eightfold Path. The eight components of the Path (right view, right aspiration, right speech, right doing, right livelihood, right effort, right mindfulness, right concentration) are reduced to (i) discipline in morality (ii) discipline in meditation, and (iii) discipline in higher insight, and tradition has elaborated each of these stages of discipline in great detail. The discipline of meditation involves use of various devices for concentration such as fixing on a certain colour, recollections of the Buddha, the Dharma, and the Sangha, and attention to breathing.

Partly for the sake of a contrast to be brought out below, the following comment will be of interest. The writer is speaking of one aspect of discipline in morality, namely a monk's use of his meagre possessions:

> Upon this . . . a more liberal construction may be put: we can interpret it in terms of a wise and thoughtful use of all material possessions. Nevertheless for the householder, cumbered as he is with all manner of worldly goods and gear, the principle will be much more difficult of application than for the homeless and well-nigh possessionless wanderer, especially as the former often happens to have so many things for which the only use is an unwise one. How much more difficult for him therefore the practice of Meditation!(5).

Study of Torah on the other hand involves learning, reciting and dialectical discussion of certain texts, especially of the Talmud. Rabbi Johanan ben Zakkai said: 'If thou hast wrought much in the study of Torah take no credit to thyself, for to this end wast thou created'(6). With this, incidentally and for contrast with the passage from Bhikshu Sangharakshita above, it is interesting to put a saying of Rabban Gamaliel, the son of Judah the Prince: 'Splendid is the study of Torah when combined with a worldly occupation'(7).

With regard to the institutional actions mentioned earlier, it is

51

reasonably clear that there are bound to be a number of incompatibilities in particular cases. Could a given individual $M$, living in Bangkok or Jerusalem or Des Moines, be both a monk and a rabbi? Some of these incompatibilities are due to such physical facts as the geographical locations of temples, shrines and synagogues. A more important consideration is the social significance of these courses of action, which is not something extrinsic to them, something which they might or might not have; their social meaning is built into their very structure.

Many years ago at a conference on Christian unity a Protestant speaker told how he had come to appreciate certain features of various Churches. The way he put it was that he had become a Catholic, and then he had become a Presbyterian, and then a Baptist, and so on. But everyone knew that all the while he was really a member of the Disciples of Christ, and that he had become a Catholic, etc., only in a manner of speaking. He was not really a member in good standing of any of the other Churches, because the set of institutional actions he was actually carrying out in his career identified him as a Disciple.

Just as we could construct hypothetical cases where B-actions, or conjunctions of them, would be incompatible with J-actions, or conjunctions of them, for a certain individual to perform, we could construct contrasting courses of action which it would be impossible for anyone to carry out jointly.

Suppose for the sake of argument that the Dharma taught that a celibate life conduces more to the extinction of cravings and thus to attainment of Nirvana than a married life does, but that a married life does not make attainment of Nirvana absolutely impossible. Even granting that for some people marriage is better on the whole, somewhat as Aquinas grants that, though the contemplative life is better absolutely, the active life is better for some people. And suppose that according to the Torah one can respond to God more fully and completely in a married life than in a celibate one, though one can respond rightly to God in a limited way without marrying.

In that case we would not yet have sufficient reason for saying that B3 and J3 recommend incompatible courses of action, though we would have learned something about some contrasting (and possibly opposed) valuations they involve. For in this case

52

the contrasting patterns of life do not require incompatible actions, though they may involve opposed valuations and beliefs.

Suppose on the contrary, again for the sake of argument, that the Dharma taught that celibacy is necessary for the attainment of Nirvana and that the Torah taught that marriage is necessary for responding rightly to God. Then the contrasting patterns of life would require incompatible courses of action and recommendations of these patterns of life would be in opposition in that way. For no one could then accept both B3 and J3 without involving himself in an absurdity; he would be undertaking two courses of action which cannot be carried out together.

The question remains just what specific courses of action different religions do actually require for the comprehensive courses of action which are embedded in their patterns of life. But this is not the kind of question a philosopher should speak to, or that he needs to speak to.

One interesting point is that the rules of different religions governing specific courses of action may not have exactly the same range of coverage. There may be some situations which both B-rules and J-rules cover, but there may be other situations which one or both of these sets of rules fail to cover. Oppositions of doctrines which recommend specific courses of action could occur only with respect to situations where both doctrines are relevant. For example, if neither religion has any specific rules about corporate finance, or if only one does, then obviously there would be no opposition of practical doctrines on that point.

Now we can sum up on what it would mean to say of a pair of doctrines of different religions, which have the force of recommending courses of action, that they are opposed. Let us notice first how courses of action are incompatible, and then what it means to accept a recommendation.

A comprehensive course of action is a pattern of action which characterises a whole of life. It seems that such courses of action are being recommended in B2.2 and J2.2 But comprehensive courses of action have to be distinguished from general orientations to life. Someone might have a general orientation to life, involving certain valuations and beliefs, without having a comprehensive course of action. Then we would say that his pattern

53

of life is not a practical way of life. We might be inclined to say that he has a philosophy of life.

The major religions of the world seem to embody in their patterns of life not only general orientations to life, in the form of complexes of valuations and beliefs, but also courses of action. They offer practical ways of life. Their doctrines propose valuations of actual and possible existents, and beliefs about existents and the conditions of existence. But their doctrines also recommend specific courses of action which are built into the structures of comprehensive courses of action such as those recommended in B2.2 and J2.2. The normative bodies of teaching referred to in B3 and J3, the Dharma and the Torah, include specific rules for action as well as general rules.

A course of action is a series of connected actions. So two courses of action are incompatible if some action which is a member of one is incompatible with some action which is a member of the other. Two actions are incompatible for some agent if for some reason or other it is impossible for him to perform both of them. Two actions are incompatible without restriction if no one can perform both of them. The reasons why someone cannot perform both actions may have to do with the way things are in his environment, including very general conditions of existence, or they may be facts about his own constitution. Now if two actions are incompatible, then courses of action of which the actions are members are also incompatible. Both courses of action cannot be carried out. And if two specific courses of action, which are incompatible, are required by different comprehensive courses of action, then these comprehensive courses of action could not be carried out jointly. Further, if two comprehensive courses of action cannot be carried out jointly, then the patterns of life in which they are ingredients are incompatible for joint realisation.

Now let us see what it means to accept a recommendation of a course of action. Accepting a recommendation is more than acknowledging that it has been made and that it is a valid recommendation, i.e. that the programme is (i) free from internal inconsistency, (ii) *prima facie* consistent with the known conditions of the situation, and (iii) relevant to the situation. Acknowledging that the programme is a real possibility, that it might be

54

adopted by the hearer, would not count as accepting the recommendation.

We can compare this with what it means to accept a proposal for belief. Accepting a proposal for belief means more than acknowledging that the proposal has been made and that it is a valid proposal for belief, i.e. that what is proposed for belief is (i) free from internal inconsistency, (ii) *prima facie* consistent with what is known about the subject-matter (i.e., it is plausible), and (iii) relevant to the situation. In other words, acknowledging that the belief is a real possibility would not be counted as accepting the proposal for belief.

Accepting a proposal for belief means more than this; it means judging that what is proposed (the proposition, exploiting the term a little) is true and expressing this judgement in agreement with the proposal. Similarly but with differences to be brought out further later on, accepting a recommendation means adopting it, that is undertaking to carry out what is recommended and expressing this undertaking in agreement with the recommendation.

So accepting both of two course-of-action recommendations would mean adopting both of them, that is to say undertaking to carry out both of the courses of action. But suppose the courses of action are incompatible. Then one would be undertaking to do what in fact cannot be done. This might be characterised as undertaking an absurd course of action, or it might be characterised as acting inconsistently. In this case the two course-of-action recommendations cannot be accepted jointly without absurdity. So the doctrines which make these recommendations are opposed.

We can be mistaken as to whether a course of action is really impossible or not. On the one hand sometimes we say: I thought it couldn't be done, but he did it. On the other hand sometimes we say: I tried, but I discovered that I was trying to do the impossible. Hence absurdities in making and accepting course-of-action recommendations are by no means always obvious; indeed the obvious absurdities are not the dangerous ones. All of us commit these absurdities unknowingly from time to time, and sometimes we discover what we have done.

Hence we can be mistaken as to whether some pair of course-

55

of-action recommendations are opposed or not. But if we have good reason to believe that it is really impossible to carry out both courses of action then we have good reason to believe that the doctrines recommending them are opposed.

Following up the comparison of recommendations with proposals for belief above, this would be a good place to consider some of the kinds of assertions that are associated with course-of-action recommendations, in anticipation of the next two chapters.

To any recommendation of a course of action there corresponds a possible assertion to the effect that the course of action is being carried out, that the addressee is acting in the recommended manner. Thus if the recommendations B3 and J3 are made, then on later occasions assertions of the following forms might be made.

——— is living in accord with the Dharma.
——— is living in accord with the Torah.

From these schemas we obtain sentences by filling in the blanks with terms which refer to the addressees of the recommendations. Thus if B3 is addressed to $M$ and J3 is addressed to $N$ we would have:

$M$ is living in accord with the Dharma.
$N$ is living in accord with the Torah.

Assertions of these sentences are consistent with one another, whether or not the recommendations B3 and J3 are in opposition.

Now suppose that B3 and J3 were both addressed to the same individual $M$. Then we would have:

$M$ is living in accord with the Dharma.
$M$ is living in accord with the Torah.

Now if B3 and J3 are not opposed to one another, assertions of these sentences are consistent with one another. But if the courses of action are incompatible and hence the recommendations are opposed, assertions of these sentences would be inconsistent with one another.

We may or may not wish to say the recommendations themselves are inconsistent with one another. We may wish to save 'consistent' and 'inconsistent' for indicative sentences or for propositions or for assertions. In any case it is natural to say

56

that if anyone recommends incompatible courses of action to someone (without knowing they are incompatible, we would ordinarily suppose), he is acting inconsistently, and that if anyone undertakes to carry out incompatible courses of action he is acting inconsistently. Further, if we should construe indicative sentences or propositions as forms of possible assertions this would encourage applying 'consistent' and 'inconsistent' to recommendations also. For in that case, in saying that $p$ and $q$ are inconsistent we would be saying that anyone who asserts both $p$ and $q$ is acting inconsistently. In this respect, though not in others, oppositions of recommendations and oppositions of assertions would be in the same boat.

In recommending a course of action a speaker is not of course committed to assertions like those above. His recommendations may not be accepted. But he is indeed committed to assertions of another sort, to the effect that what he recommends is possible. If anyone recommends a course of action he supposes it can be carried out, and if anyone undertakes a course of action he too supposes it can be carried out, though of course either or both can be wrong about this. These are existential suppositions, about physical states of affairs or the constitutions and characters of human beings or other conditions of existence including very general ones. If the relevant conditions do not hold, then in recommending or undertaking the course of action we are committing an absurdity, usually unknowingly. We are recommending that someone should do, or we are undertaking to do, something which is in fact impossible.

Most of these suppositions are just that – suppositions. They are taken for granted, not deliberately asserted. But if the validity of the recommendation or the reasonableness of adopting it are challenged, assertions of the relevant suppositions, and defences of them, are called for.

What has been said so far is true of commands and requests as well as of recommendations. But for recommendations something more is required. The speaker is responsible not only for assertions to the effect that the course of action is possible but for further assertions to the effect that it is a reasonable thing to do. Showing the course of action is possible is showing the recommendation can be adopted. But a recommender is not just saying it can be

57

adopted; he is saying it should be adopted. Thus he is committed to saying that in view of the circumstances the course of action is a reasonable thing to do, or even perhaps *the* reasonable thing to do.

This is not true of commands and requests. (Often in practice a *prima facie* command is only a strong recommendation, though the speaker may be ready to turn it into a pure command if necessary. Also speakers are often willing to retreat from commands to recommendations if compliance is not forthcoming.) Though it would be absurd to command something which cannot be done, it is possible without absurdity to give a command without being responsible for giving reasons (other than threats or promises) why the course of action should be carried out. The giver of a command may be unreasonable in the sense that he is being unjust or inhumane or even arbitrary, but what he is doing is not absurd. He wants something done and he is telling someone to do it. Theirs not to reason why.

But it is not possible without absurdity to make a recommendation without being ready and willing to give reasons why it should be adopted. Now speakers in $S$ are not in a position to command when they present practical doctrines, since none is in a position of authority relative to others; they can at most recommend courses of action. This means they are committed to making assertions which go beyond showing a course of action is possible. They are responsible for showing it would be a good thing to do. Hence their assertions have to include positive valuations of experiences, states and objects which would be involved in the course of action. We consider these in the next chapter.

Sometimes when we are confronted with a pair of opposed assertions we accept one or the other, but often we decide, reasonably, to accept neither. (i) Sometimes we decide that both of them are untrue. We decide that the height of the arch is neither ten feet nor twenty feet, or that neither of two opposed physical theories is adequate to the facts. Or (ii) we decide that we are not in a position to decide the question one way or another. From where one stands it is too far to tell how high the arch is; it is too early to tell how the physical theories would work out. We decide the situation calls for suspension of judgement. So the

58

only obligation imposed on us by an opposition of assertions is to recognise that *if* we accept one of them we cannot accept the other.

This applies to opposed course-of-action recommendations as well. We decide to go neither to Boston nor to New York but to Northampton, or to stay at home. Or we decide to consider the matter further. Again the only limitation imposed on us is to recognise that if we undertake to carry out one of the incompatible courses of action we cannot undertake the other.

Now apply this to the utterances we have been discussing. Suppose (i) that B2–3 and J2–3 express central practical doctrines of Buddhism and of Judaism respectively and (ii) that they recommend incompatible courses of action and therefore are in opposition. Then what would follow from these suppositions is not that one must be either a Buddhist or a Jew but only that one cannot be both a Buddhist and a Jew. An opposition is not necessarily a dilemma. But I have not argued that practical doctrines of Buddhism and of Judaism are in fact in opposition. My object has been only to show by use of a hypothetical case what it would mean for practical doctrines of different religions to be opposed to one another.

# 5    Proposals of Valuations

In this chapter we study utterances of religious doctrines in $S$ which have the force of proposing valuations. A valuation is a judgement that something or other, for example some occasion of experience or some existent object, is good or bad in a certain way. Some of the distinctions between different types of valuations made by C. I. Lewis will be useful, especially later on. (*a*) An utterance ascribing intrinsic value to something says it is good for its own sake, as an end in itself. Lewis thinks judgements of this type apply only to 'the content of some actual or possible experience'. (*b*) An utterance ascribing inherent value to something says it is 'good without reference to any further object', since an intrinsic value is findable in its presence. Judgements of this type apply to actual or possible existents including states of affairs. (*c*) An utterance ascribing contributory value to something says that it contributes in some way to some intrinsic value (1).

Generally speaking, when someone recommends a course of action he implies a valuation of some object involved in the course of action or some quality intrinsic to the course of action or some outcome of the course of action. Also, when he gives reasons for carrying out the course of action these include valuations, for in recommending the course of action the speaker is saying it would be a good thing to do. Thus in recommending and giving reasons for the course of action the speaker implies valuations of his own; also he is proposing that the addressee should value something in a certain way.

Ordinarily a speaker does not propose that the addressee should make exactly the same set of valuations which he himself is making. $M$ may hope that in carrying out the course of action $N$ will discover values of which he ($M$) may not be aware; and this would reveal one of $M$'s own moral valuations. But when a

60

speaker recommends a course of action he cannot avoid proposing, explicitly or implicitly, some of the valuations he himself is making.

Clearly this holds for religious discourse, as we saw in the last chapter. The development from B2/J2 to B2.3/J2.3 in our problematical case showed how recommendations of comprehensive courses of action involve orientations to life and distinctive sorts of valuations. These are built directly into the comprehensive courses of action; no one could undertake these courses of action without making these valuations. Also religious doctrines build valuations into the structure of some specific courses of action. No one could perform specific acts of worship without valuing God in a certain way, and no one could practise meditation according to the Dharma without valuing and re-valuing, negatively, perceptual and imaginative experiences in certain ways. If anyone recommends these courses of action he must be proposing the valuations also. Further, the reasons the speaker must be ready and willing to give for carrying them out must include assertions of valuations, and asserting a valuation to someone means proposing that he should make that same valuation himself. So if the doctrines of the major religions present practical ways of life, as they certainly seem to do, some of their doctrines must have the force of proposing valuations.

Reacting to scientific and historical criticisms of traditional religious beliefs, many modern Western theologians and religious philosophers have stressed the importance of valuations in religion and even exaggerated their importance. On the other hand critical philosophers of religion have not studied religious valuations as much as they should. Rudolf Otto's study of 'the holy' as a category of valuation (2) was a seminal development, and among others Ninian Smart has made some important contributions (3). But it seems fair to say that, generally speaking, philosophers have devoted far less attention to religious valuations than to moral valuations and aesthetic valuations. A number of recent developments, including studies in the logic of preference (4), could be exploited fruitfully in studies of valuations in religious discourse (5).

Our immediate object is to see how utterances of B2–3 and J2–3 in $S$ could be opposed by virtue of valuations they convey and propose. But some general considerations about how proposals of valuations can be opposed might help to focus on the problem.

An utterance which proposes a valuation to someone does not just reveal or report the fact that the speaker himself makes the valuation, that he regards or takes something as good or bad in a certain way, though ordinarily this is a fair inference. The speaker is proposing that the hearer should regard or take something as good or bad in a certain way.

Now some valuations are incompatible with others. No one can regard something as both good in a certain way and also bad in that way. Also, in the case of the comparative valuations involved in preferences, no one can rank $x$ over $y$ in a certain way and also rank $y$ over $x$ in that way. And if someone should rank $x$ over $y$ and $y$ over $z$ and then fail to rank $x$ over $z$, he would be acting inconsistently. Further, along with these incompatibilities of positive/negative valuations and of comparative valuations, some positive valuations are incompatible with other positive valuations. No one can take something as uniquely good in a certain way and also take something else as uniquely good in that way, for example. So two proposals of valuations are opposed if the valuations are incompatible somehow or other; in that case the proposals are not jointly acceptable, for accepting a proposal means making the valuation, regarding or taking something as good or bad in the way proposed, and accepting a pair of opposed proposals would mean making two incompatible valuations.

Valuations are not incompatible in the same ways courses of action are. For example, we would not wish to say that valuations are physically incompatible, though we would say this of some pairs of courses of action. In this respect valuations are closer to beliefs. On the other hand valuations are not incompatible in just the same way beliefs are, for one's valuation of something is not just a deduction from one's beliefs about it. So we need to consider oppositions of proposals of valuations as well as oppositions of course-of-action recommendations and oppositions of proposals for belief.

Consider B2 (Aim at attaining Nirvana) and J2 (Respond rightly to God) together with the developments of these in B2.2–3 and J2.2–3. Implicit in these are valuations of something to which life as a whole or on the whole or above all is being oriented. The forms of these valuations can be developed as follows.

If someone makes the valuation conveyed in the B-series we could assert of him something of the following form:

B2a*  $M$ is valuing attainment of Nirvana as ———.

And if someone else makes the valuation conveyed in the J-series we could assert of him something of the following form:

J2a*  $N$ is valuing God as ———.

In each case, to complete the assertion we would need to fill in the blank with an appropriate expression. The conditions for appropriate expressions are: (i) that the expression should be congruent with the character of what is being valued, in B2a* Nirvana and in J2a* God, and hence expressive of the manner of directing life which is being recommended, in the B-series a teleological manner and in the J-series a responsive manner; and (ii) that the expression should convey the force of the qualifiers 'as a whole' or 'on the whole' or 'above all' and thus assign a certain primacy to what is being valued.

Thus by (i) 'the lord of life' would not fit well into B2a* and 'the supreme attainable state' would be out of place in J2a*, under standard senses of 'Nirvana' and 'God'. But 'the supreme goal of life' would fit into B2a*, since it expresses an aim and since it gives Nirvana primacy over other goals. And 'holy' in the sense developed by Otto (something is holy if it is both a *mysterium tremendum et fascinans* and schematisable by rational concepts) would be suitable for J2a*, since it evokes a responsive attitude in the strong sense of 'responsive' mentioned earlier and since it marks off God from all other existents and assigns a transcendent value.

So, though other expressions might be equally appropriate let us use these to complete B2a* and J2a* into:

B2a  $M$ is valuing attainment of Nirvana as the supreme goal of life.

J2a  $N$ is valuing God as holy.

Now if these assertions are true of $M$ and $N$ we could expect them to be willing to utter the following on appropriate occasions:

B2v Nirvana is the supreme goal of life.
J2v God is holy.

Then one way to ask whether B2 and J2 are opposed is to ask whether we could say consistently of some one person both what is said of $M$ in B2a and what is said of $N$ in J2a. And this is to ask whether one and the same person could assert B2v and J2v without absurdity, without acting inconsistently. For if no one could assert both B2v and J2v without absurdity, then proposals of these two valuations are in opposition.

When a speaker proposes a valuation he is recommending that his hearer should review his present estimation of some object or quality or end. He is also doing something more than this. What more is he doing? He wishes a certain outcome of this review; he would like the hearer to change his estimate. Now what can he do about this in saying what he says? What more must be said in the utterance of a proposal of a valuation?

Since the valuation cannot be commanded in $S$ or in any other situation but only proposed, it seems that, if what is said in the utterance is to bear on the desired change in estimation (that is, to go beyond a recommendation to review), the utterance must assert something of the object or quality or end in question. It may do this indirectly by asserting something of the hearer in relation to the object or quality or end, but this cannot be done without implying some assertion about the object or quality or end itself. For when a speaker proposes that someone should value something $m$ in a certain way the proposal must carry with it an implicit assertion that $m$ deserves to be valued in that way.

Indeed the most natural way to convey and propose a valuation is in the form of an assertion. Consider the difference between these two formulas where 'V' stands for some value-predicate or other:

f1 I propose that you value $m$ as V.
f2 $m$ is V.

Normally and certainly in $S$ the simpler form f2 is better than f1 because it conveys more explicitly the speaker's own valuation of *m*. This counts for f2 because there is something very peculiar and dubious about proposing to someone else a valuation one does not make oneself, at least for ascriptions of intrinsic or inherent value. There would be an absurdity in uttering a conjunction of f1 with 'I do not regard *m* as V', reminiscent of Moore's paradox: '*p* but I do not believe that *p*'. A speaker can consistently recommend a specific course of action which, because of a difference in circumstances, he himself does not intend to carry out. But he cannot consistently propose a valuation which he himself does not make. In this respect proposals of valuations are like proposals for belief and unlike course-of-action recommendations. A second advantage to f2 is this: the fact that the utterance is a proposal is normally manifest in the context, so making this explicit as in f1 can be misleading, suggesting some hidden reason for explicating what is obvious, or sounding as though valuing something is doing something in the wrong sense of 'doing'.

Now coming back to B2v and J2v, how could these proposals of valuations be in opposition? Later we can consider proposals of valuations of other types.

Nirvana is often spoken of as a state which can be realised and enjoyed. It is said to be bliss. Certainly it would not be characterised as an emotional state. Perhaps it would not be characterised as a state of mind either. 'A state of being'? Objections might be raised to this too: Nirvana is beyond being and non-being – which is sometimes said of God also. But Nirvana is certainly spoken of in different ways than God is spoken of, so one must fumble for some way of indicating roughly a contrast between the concepts. This is not to legislate how anyone should speak of Nirvana, especially not how Buddhists should. If Nirvana is indeed a state which can be realised and enjoyed, we can say in Lewis's terminology that B2v ascribes intrinsic value to attainment of Nirvana. It says this is good in itself. And if God is construed as an actual existent (with whatever qualifications are needed to avoid 'idolatry'), since God can be obeyed and otherwise responded to, then we can say that J2v ascribes inherent value to God. In the presence of God intrinsic values can be found. Then are these proposals jointly acceptable, or not? As in the case of B1 and J1 the answer is not obvious, not only because common terms are lacking but

65

also because B2v and J2v propose valuations of different types. Nevertheless there are two ways in which an opposition could be located if it exists. One is by considering the references involved in B2v and J2v; the other is by considering their predications.

If a term is employed in a referential way and not as some terms are used in myths, fairy tales and poetry, the speaker should be willing to explicate and defend the reference by establishing some starting-point in experience, and by articulating some conceptual network, however rudimentary, by aid of which the reference can move from its starting-point to its goal. If no starting-point in experience can be established or if the conceptual network is inappropriate or misconstructed, the reference will fail. Thus we ordinarily suppose that references to Thor's hammer, elves who make shoes, and phlogiston will fail for various reasons.

Suppose B2v were conjoined with 'There is no such thing as God' or that J2v were conjoined with 'There is no such thing as Nirvana'. This would be a short and easy way of finding an opposition. But, since we are concerned with oppositions of positive teachings of different religions, this would be too short and easy unless these negatives, which deny that successful references are possible, were derived from positive doctrines in the B-series and in the J-series.

So the question is whether we could construct hypothetical cases where some doctrine which is required for the success of a reference in B2v, or on which B2v depends in some other way, implies a failure of reference to God, or where some doctrine on which J2v depends, either for a reference or otherwise, implies a failure of reference to Nirvana. Hypothetical cases, cases where we consider what would happen if $B$ and $J$ developed their doctrines in certain ways, are all we need since our object is not to show that certain doctrines actually taught by different religions are in fact in opposition to one another but only to show how oppositions of doctrines of different religions might occur. If we can construct such cases for B2v and J2v this would show how those doctrines might come into opposition by virtue of the references they involve, assuming of course that 'Nirvana' and 'God' are being used referentially.

66

Consider the assertion that all beings are subject to becoming and perishing. And suppose (a) that B2v requires this assertion as a necessary starting-point in experience for understanding what is being referred to as Nirvana. Or suppose (b) that B2v requires this assertion in some other way, so that if it were not true then B2v would not be a valid proposal. Now suppose also that in explication of J2v God would be referred to as the being who is not subject to becoming and perishing. Then in both cases the validity of B2v depends on an assertion which implies a failure of reference to God, and in the a-case the success of a reference to Nirvana implies the failure of a reference to God. Thus in either case B2v and J2v would be opposed.

Consider some other cases, centring about an assertion that no human action can be genuinely effective without the power of God. Suppose (a) that in constructing a reference to God in explication of J2v it is necessary to start from an implication of this, namely that no human action can be independently effective. God is that power without which our actions cannot be effective. Or suppose (b) that J2v requires this assertion, that no human action can be effective without the power of God, for its validity in some other way. Now suppose also that in explication of B2v it would be necessary, for the sake of developing a reference to Nirvana, to assert that Nirvana is a state attainable by strictly independent human action. For if it were not, the argument might run, it would be a conditioned state and that is not the sort of thing one is referring to when one speaks of Nirvana. Then in both cases the validity of J2v depends on an assertion which implies a failure of reference to Nirvana, and in the a-case the success of a reference to God implies a failure of reference to Nirvana. Again in both cases B2v and J2v would be opposed.

Of course in the relevant literatures it is not so simple. These are thorny and complicated issues and they have been treated by extremely subtle minds, so that historical and comparative studies of these matters would have to be highly ramified.

Notice that in the two a-cases we would have not just different references but antagonistic references. The referential power of one utterance would nullify that of the other. And this would bring B2v and J2v into opposition for they would not be jointly acceptable. It would be impossible for anyone without absurdity to

67

ascribe the values proposed, or indeed any other values, to both referents, because the references themselves are incompatible.

In the two b-cases B2v and J2v would still be in opposition but in a somewhat different way. Instead of a direct conflict between references we would have conflicts between the references involved in one proposal and some essential doctrines about the referent in the other proposal. In both the a-cases and the b-cases, if we could apply 'true' to ascriptions of value, we could say that B2v and J2v cannot both be true. No one can make these valuations jointly without absurdity.

If we attend to the predications in B2v and J2v, instead of to the references they involve, we may find ourselves sensing oppositions or the possibility of them in a different way. And these oppositions, arising from the values being ascribed in their predications, may throw more light on religious valuations, since oppositions by virtue of references to logical subjects can occur between non-valuational assertions as well. I shall discuss two ways in which such distinctively valuational oppositions could be brought out, if they exist. One way is by deriving from B2v and J2v valuations with homogeneous references and the same restricted primacy-ranking predicate. The other way is by construing their predicates as expressing unrestricted primacy-rankings. Hopefully these dark sayings will begin to make some sense as we go along.

At least on their surface the referents in B2v and J2v are heterogeneous; it seems they would fall under different categories, that different modes of existence are involved. It seems that Nirvana is an attainable state and that God is an actual existent. That is one reason why the two valuations are not obviously opposed. For suppose that each predicate is taken to assign to its subject a primacy within some category. Then B2v's predicate assigns primacy to Nirvana in the category of attainable goals and J2v's predicate assigns a primacy to God in the category of actual existents. In this case the predicates have the force of restricted primacy-rankings. Then it is not clearly true that these valuations are in opposition. There is no inconsistency in ranking some $m$ first in one category and ranking some $n$ first in some other category.

But suppose one could derive from this pair of valuations,

which have heterogeneous references, another pair of valuations with homogeneous references, references in the same mode of existence, and a predicate which assigns primacy within this category. Then an opposition could occur. One cannot award primacy in the same category to both *m* and *n*. And if the second pair are indeed derived from the first pair, then the first pair would be in opposition also.

For example, if the doctrines in the J-series were developed in a certain way we could find a reference to an attainable state which might be described as adhesion to God (*devekuth*) (6). Suppose the Torah were thought to teach that the right response to God is to seek, above all other goals, to attain this state. Then this would permit pairing B2v with a valuation in the same category as follows:

B2v (Attainment of) Nirvana is the supreme goal of life.
J2v' (Attainment of) adhesion to God is the supreme goal of life.

Now both of these valuations cannot be made without absurdity, since the common predicate assigns a primacy, unless the two references converge to an identical referent. No one could value one state as the supreme goal of life and also value a different state as the supreme goal of life. And if J2v' did follow from J2v, that is if the holiness of God did call for this kind of response, then this would bring J2v into indirect opposition with B2v.

Similarly if the doctrines of the B-series were devoloped in a certain direction it might be possible to derive a reference to the subject of a valuation which would be comparable, at least, to references to God. This possibility is suggested by various Mahayana developments of Buddhist doctrines. Consider the following passages from the writings of Professor Masao Abe:

In Buddhism, Buddha or the Awakened One, whose nature is said to be held by everyone, is none other than one who realizes that which is 'even more interior to me than my own interior' [a quotation from Augustine] as the Absolute Nothingness, and thus as one's True Self which is the ground of oneself and of the world. . . . The Buddhist idea of identity is

69

not an identity with the ultimate as 'God' who is *hāyāh*, *Sein*, *esse ipsum* or whatever it may be called, but an identity with the Ultimate as the 'Absolute Nothingness' which, as Realization, is named Nirvana, *Sūnyata*, the Non-discriminating wisdom or *jinen* (7).

The Ground of our existence is nothingness, Sunyata, because it can never be objectified. This Sunyata is deep enough to encompass even God, the 'object' of mystical union as well as the object of faith. For Sunyata is not the nothingness from which God created everything but the nothingness from which God Himself emerged. Sunyata is the very ground of the self and thereby the ground of everything to which we are related (7a).

In the same article he quotes the following verses by Hakuin, the Zen Master:

What now is there to seek?
With Nirvana revealed before you,
This very place is the Lotus land,
This very body is Buddha (8).

Attainment of Nirvana is interpreted here as realisation of the Buddha-nature common to everyone, which is one's True Self. Though there are problems about reference to the True Self, and also of course about reference to God, it seems reasonably clear that in these passages the two referents are being treated as comparable. It seems that inherent value is being ascribed to the True Self, and this judgement is recognised as comparable with judgements ascribing inherent value to God. Also a common predicate is available, namely 'the ground of oneself and of the world', and it seems clear that this could be said of either referent but not of both. So we could arrive at the following pair of incompatible valuations:

Bgv The True Self is the ground of oneself and of the world.
Jgv God is the ground of oneself and of the world.

As in the former case these valuations cannot be made jointly without absurdity unless their referents are identical, and the author of the passages above stresses that they are not. So proposals of them would be in opposition.

It could be argued that Bgv and Jgv express beliefs, not valuations. This issue might turn on how 'the ground of' could be explicated. I do not doubt that beliefs about existents and the conditions of existence are involved in Bgv and Jgv but it could be argued that valuations are involved also, in the following way. We might say that 'the ground of oneself . . .' assigns a primacy within the class of entities on which we depend in some way or other. But what one says one depends on will itself depend on how one identifies oneself, and identifying oneself in this context would seem to involve valuations. However that may be, whether this case belongs here or in Chapter 6 where we deal with proposals for belief, it seems a clear case of opposition by virtue of a uniquely-applying predicate.

So far we have been exploring one possible strategy for tracking down suspected oppositions between proposals of valuations which have heterogeneous referents. Faced with a pair of such valuations that strategy would be: (i) to take the value-predicates as ascribing a primacy in value within some category; (ii) to examine the doctrinal schemes in which the valuations are embedded to see whether a pair of homogeneous references could be formulated; and (iii) to find a primacy-ranking value predicate which could be said of either referent, but not of both without absurdity.

There is another way of dealing with the problem of the heterogeneity of references and thus another way of telling whether valuation-proposals are opposed by virtue of their predications. That is by seeing whether the doctrinal schemes give the predicates an unrestricted primacy-ranking force, or whether the predicates are uniquely-applying without restriction in some other manner. For if this should be the case the heterogeneity of the references would not matter. The force of the predicate would be to rank some referent over anything else whatsoever, whether a goal or an actual existent or something of any other category one might choose. The point is not that the use of the unrestricted predicate would abolish categories of referents; rather, it would subordinate to some referent all other things in all categories.

Anselm's *quo maius nihil cogitari potest* is a predicate whose

71

unrestricted primacy-ranking force is clear and explicit. Its valuational character – and this is not by any means to say that his argument is just a set of value judgements – comes out even more clearly as he develops his thought in the following passages:

And You, Lord our God, are this being. You exist so truly, Lord my God, that You cannot even be thought not to exist. And this is as it should be, for if some intelligence could think of something better [*melius*] than You, the creature would be above its creator and would judge its creator – and that is completely absurd. In fact, everything else there is, except You alone, can be thought of as not existing. You alone, then, of all things most truly exist and therefore of all things possess existence to the highest degree; for anything else does not exist as truly, and so possesses existence to a lesser degree.

What then are You, Lord God, You than whom nothing greater can be thought? But what are You save that supreme being, existing through Yourself alone, who made everything else from nothing? . . . What goodness, then, could be wanting to the supreme good, through which every good exists? Thus You are just, truthful, happy, and whatever it is better to be than not to be. . . . (9)

Now consider the possibility that the predicate of B2v, 'the supreme goal of life', and that of J2v 'holy', might each have a similar unrestricted primacy-ranking force. The way Nirvana is spoken of in the literature of Theravada Buddhism strongly suggests that Nirvana is being ranked not only above other goals in life but above anything else whatsoever, including all actual existents. Thus whereas all existents are in flux and subject to perishing – and hence the *anatta* doctrine which denies that the soul or self is substantial and permanent, Nirvana is the unborn, the unageing, the undecaying, the undying, the unsorrowing, the stainless, the uttermost security from the bonds (10). (The abundance of adjectives itself suggests a superlative valuation.) The Buddha is 'the Blessed One' because of his attainment of Nirvana and the wisdom and force of his teachings (the Dharma)

72

which show the path to Nirvana. The gods are plentiful and have important parts to play in the stories. For example, after his enlightenment the Buddha is disinclined to teach *dhamma*, but Brahmā Sahampati appears before him and persuades him to do so out of compassion (11). Yet they also rank below the attainment of Nirvana in religious importance. The king of the gods bows down before the arhat (12), who has attained Nirvana.

Similarly the literatures of Judaism and other theistic religions abound in superlatives which have the effect of ranking God above all else, above any creature and any state attainable by any creature. In many of its uses 'holy' has this force. The doctrine that God is the creator of all things and the King of the Universe gives a structural framework and support for this valuation. With it go the precepts to love God with all our heart and with all our soul and with all our might, and to obey his law in all we do.

Now if the doctrinal schemes to which B2v and J2v belong give these predicates an unrestricted primacy-ranking force, then B2v and J2v are opposed. It would not be enough if only one of the predicates had this force. Giving something primacy in some category, for example ranking human beings in value above all other animals or above all other created things, is compatible with giving something else an unrestricted primacy. We could express the difference between (1) restricted and (2) unrestricted primacy-ranking valuations by the formulas:

(1)  $(\exists x)\,(Fx) \cdot (y)\,(Fy \supset Rxy)$.
(2)  $(\exists x)\,(y)\,(Rxy)$.

But if both predicates have this latter force then incompatible valuations are being proposed and no one could accept both proposals. The same thing would be true if the predicates of B2v and J2v were uniquely-applying in some other way than by having an unrestricted primacy-ranking force.

I have dwelled on B2v and J2v because valuations of this type are particularly important in the structures of doctrines in the major religions and in the activities and experiences which affect the developments of doctrines. They have some right to be called basic religious valuations, for if we look on doctrinal schemes as presenting patterns of life such a valuation tells us what some

73

scheme of doctrines places at the centre of the orientation to life it recommends. We have studied how proposals of these valuations can be opposed (1) if one doctrine implies a failure of the reference in the other, or (2) if their predications are incompatible. In either sort of case the valuations proposed are incompatible and hence the proposals are in opposition.

Before going on to valuations of other types it is worth recalling that all these derivations of oppositions are hypothetical. They do not say what doctrines an adherent of a certain tradition ought, from what we know of the tradition, to teach. The object is only to see how oppositions of doctrines of different religions are possible. So the conclusions of our derivations have the following force: If $M$ utters $u_1$ and $N$ utters $u_2$ in $S$, if these are utterances of doctrines of different religions, and if their doctrinal schemes make it fair to construe $u_1$ and $u_2$ in certain ways, then $u_1$ and $u_2$ are opposed. So when two utterances are not patently opposed, derivations of oppositions from them are contingent on the characters of the doctrinal schemes to which they belong. I do not claim to have stated correctly the doctrines of any religion. The sentences I use have been suggested by the literatures of various religions but suggestions are not made of the same stuff as conclusions. All I hope is that they are plausible enough to be instructive.

Valuations of a different type are implicit in the recommendations of comprehensive courses of action B3 (Live in accord with the Dharma) and J3 (Live in accord with the Torah). In each case the recommendation conveys an ascription of value to a whole of life, a whole composed of the multiplicity of experiences, actions and thoughts which occur in the span of a lifetime. C. I. Lewis says: 'a life good on the whole ... is something whose goodness or badness is at no moment immediately disclosed, but can be contemplated only by some imaginative or synthetic envisagement of its on-the-whole quality' (13). Given the doctrine of rebirth, this would come to mean the whole of a series of lives, a series which would come to an end if Nirvana is attained. These valuations can be formulated in the following way:

B3v   The good life is a life in accord with the Dharma.

Compare 'Even the gods envy those who are awakened and not

74

forgetful, who are given to meditation, who are wise, and who delight in the repose of retirement (from the world)' (*Dhammapada* 181, tr. Max Müller).

J3v  The good life is a life in accord with the Torah.

Compare 'Blessed is the man that walketh not in the counsel of the wicked, Nor standeth in the way of sinners, Nor sitteth in the seat of scoffers; But his delight is in the law of the Lord; and on his law doth he meditate day and night' (*Psalms* 1:1–3).

Just as B3 and J3 recommend that life should be shaped in certain ways, so B3v and J3v propose the corresponding judgements that lives shaped in these ways are good.

The best way to explain these valuations is by first introducing another type, valuations of particular occasions of experience, to which we shall come back later on. We think of some past occasions of experience and of some possible future experiences as having intrinsic value, as being good in themselves. But these experiences can be appraised as good or bad in another way as well, namely as contributing to, or as failing to contribute to or as detracting from the intrinsic value of other occasions of experience. An utterance often has both of these functions, for example, an old hymn begins: 'O happy day that fixed my choice on thee my saviour and my God.' One could read in this an ascription of contributory value to a past occasion of experience, as well as an ascription of intrinsic value. Further, particular occasions of experience can be thought of as contributing to the value of a life envisaged as a whole and shaped in accord with some pattern. Indeed it would seem that reflections on the past and anticipations of the future can yield wisdom only if valuations of past and future experiences are related to some envisagement of life as a whole. Certainly this is an ancient and perennial theme both in moral philosophy and in religious literature.

Schemes of religious doctrines generally include concepts of the good life, and the literatures of the major religions present these in vivid and concrete ways, not only in a more discursive fashion. In stories sometimes lovingly embroidered with wonderful happenings, historical or legendary figures (saints, martyrs, arhats, bodhisattvas) are celebrated and put forward as exemplars of patterns of life. Ideal virtues are developed and praised, as

75

wisdom in the book of Proverbs and love in the thirteenth chapter of I Corinthians. Ideal types of character like the 'brahmana' of the last chapter of the 'Dhammapada' and the righteous man of Psalm 15 are constructed. In these and other ways religious traditions fix attention on enduring features of character, displayed throughout many varied experiences and giving to the many experiences an enduring pattern. For it is by development of a particular set of habits of thought and action that a multiplicity of experiences are shaped into a whole of life. Comparative studies of character models in the literatures of different religious traditions would be of great interest.

How might proposals of valuations of wholes of life, such as B3v and J3v, be opposed when they are doctrines of different religions? The best way to tackle this is to clear some ground. B3v and J3v are not the same as:

B: The good life for me is a life in accord with the Dharma.
J: The good life for me is a life in accord with the Torah.

These utterances by *B* and *J* could be taken in two different ways, neither of which would give them the force of B3v and J3v.

One might construe these utterances as expressions of satisfactions actually found by the speakers in their ways of life, and not as judgements about those ways of life. The fact that *B* says this tells us that *B* is finding satisfaction in a certain whole of life, and so also for *J*. Now in so far as we take them in this way they cannot be opposed. It would be consistent for some third speaker to say both that *B* finds a satisfaction in living in accord with the Dharma and that *J* finds a satisfaction in living in accord with the Torah.

Hence B3v would not commit a speaker to disagreement with this *J*-utterance, and J3v would not commit a speaker to disagreement with this *B*-utterance if these are construed as expressions of satisfactions. B3v and J3v are appraisals of wholes of life and not (at least not just) expressions of satisfactions found in wholes of life. Recognising that a value has been found by someone, by oneself or by another, is different from appraising the experience of finding that value, i.e. the experience of having that satisfaction. So a speaker of B3v is entirely free to recognise the intrinsic satisfaction of a life in accord with the Torah which

76

is actually found by one who lives that life, and analogously for a speaker of J3v.

There is another way the *B*-utterance and the *J*-utterance could be taken: not as expressions of satisfactions actually found but as judgements in the mode of relativity to persons (14). This could be brought out by transposing 'the good life for me' into a third-person phrase: 'the good life for *M*'. Taken in this way the utterance would not be privileged in the way expressions of satisfactions are. Since these are judgements, opposed judgements by other speakers are possible. Certainly only *M* can live his life and find satisfaction in it, and it is he who must decide what whole of life he will live. But this does not rule out the possibility that he may judge wrongly about what is the best life for him to live, nor the possibility that judgements of others on this matter may deserve a hearing. The main point is that if these are judgements in the mode of relativity to persons then opposed judgements by *M* himself or by others are logically in order. One of the tangles involved in 'relativism' is caused by failure to distinguish expressions of satisfaction from value judgements in this mode.

Now the force of B3v and J3v is different from that of expressions of satisfaction and also different from that of judgements in the mode of relativity to persons. They are proposals of valuations; hence they convey and call for judgements. And they are not in the mode of relativity to persons. They purport to apply to human beings generally.

Indeed, without claiming to speak for any religion, one might venture to ask whether otherwise B3v and J3v could function as doctrines of religions, whether each could be held and taught by a community and form part of a tradition from generation to generation. And it is with doctrines of different religions that we are concerned. Certainly expressions of satisfactions are natural and very common in religious discourse. Also it is natural for a religious tradition to teach its adherents how to find religious satisfactions. But this latter point implies that its doctrines about the good life cannot themselves consist entirely in expressions of satisfactions.

Further, a religious tradition needs to teach its adherents how to make judgements about the good life in the mode of relativity

77

to persons. For a whole of life is the whole of a particular life, so in the nature of the case it must be possible for a multiplicity of wholes of life to be in accord with the Dharma or with the Torah. In practice no religion expects any two of its members to live in exactly the same way. Indeed to the very same extent that a community is effectively universal in its claims, its teachings about the good life must take account of such individual variables as physical constitutions, temperaments and occupations, and such social variables as languages, customs and laws. Hence in any well-developed body of teachings about the good life there are built-in rules for adaptations and exceptions, and principles for discriminating central from peripheral doctrines.

All this bears on how an opposition of B3v and J3v might be discussed in $S$. For the general judgements they propose must cover individual cases, and if one of them can be shown to be implausible for certain cases that would count against it. So arguments about valuations in the mode of relativity to persons (for example, valuations of the form: the good life for $M$ is a life in accord with the Dharma) would be germane to discussions of B3v and J3v.

This brings us closer to seeing how B3v and J3v could be opposed. Suppose some individual $M$ with a certain physical constitution and temperament, and with a certain personal history in a certain social environment. And suppose that B3v and J3v imply:

B3pv  The good life for $M$ is a life in accord with the Dharma.
J3pv  The good life for $M$ is a life in accord with the Torah.

Then if B3pv and J3pv are opposed this goes to show that B3v and J3v are opposed. Now B3pv and J3pv are opposed if it is not possible for $M$ to live both in accord with the Dharma and in accord with the Torah, for example if some course of action or some valuation required of him by the Dharma is incompatible with some course of action or valuation required of him by the Torah. We have seen how this might be so in discussing B3/J3 and B2v/J2v. In that case there would be an absurdity in asserting B3pv and J3pv jointly. And if these are implied by B3v and J3v respectively then there would be an absurdity in jointly asserting both of the latter.

78

However, one feels that this does not get at the heart of the matter, that for B3v and J3v to be directly and squarely opposed the synthetic character of each ought to be taken into account. Just as B3 and J3 each propose not only a list of components but a pattern in which these are interrelated in a certain way, so also B3v and J3v propose valuations of wholes in which components are interrelated in certain ways. But if their manners of putting together the elements of life are indeed different, then they must be opposed. For they are not saying just that this or that is a good life. In that case their force would be much weaker than it seems. 'The good life' means the best possible life, and this is a uniquely-applying predicate. I am not saying what a religion must teach but only that if B3v and J3v or any comparable pair of doctrines both have this force, then they are in opposition.

So far we have been treating B3v and J3v as ascriptions of intrinsic value to certain wholes of life. But we ought to take account of a further possibility also. Suppose a religion should teach that beyond any temporal whole of life there is something else, to which temporal wholes of life can contribute. Suppose that attainment of Nirvana is thought of as something beyond any temporal whole of life and so also for the Pure Land in Amida Buddhism, and for God or for 'the world to come' in Judaism. This might mean that even if temporal wholes of life have intrinsic value, a value to be found in the living of them, they have contributory value also as steps to something beyond them. Or, it might mean that temporal wholes of life have only contributory value, that a temporal life ought to be valued only as a step to something beyond it.

Then this would bring us back to the contrasts between B2 (Aim at attaining Nirvana) and J2 (Respond rightly to God) and between B2v (Nirvana is the supreme goal of life) and J2v (God is holy, or perhaps as a variant of J2v: A share in the world to come is the supreme goal of life). For ascriptions of contributory value to wholes of life would be opposed if valuations of the ends or objects to which they are said to contribute are opposed. But doctrines such as B2/J2 and B2v/J2v themselves do not have to imply that temporal wholes of life have contributory value only. Certainly one can find religious doctrines which seem to say so, but on the other hand a number of religious doctrines

79

seem to say that happiness or blessedness or a genuine fulfilment are possible in the living of a whole of life itself, even if the whole of life is also assigned a contributory value in relation to something beyond it. A religious community must have the final word about its own teachings on this point as elsewhere.

The occurrence of oppositions between those proposals of valuations of wholes of life which are doctrines of different religions would not exclude appreciation of lives lived in accord with other patterns. (i) The speaker of B3v would be free to do full justice to the integrity, the nobility and the historical value of some life lived in accord with the Torah. He is only saying that a life lived in accord with the Dharma would be better. Similarly the speaker of J3v is free to recognise the values achieved in particular lives lived in accord with the Dharma. (ii) Furthermore, each is free to recognise and appreciate the intrinsic value of another life to the person who lives it, that is to say the satisfaction that person actually finds in that whole of life, whether their appraisals of the value of finding that satisfaction are opposed or not. Thus B3v and J3v do not commit their speakers to being undiscerning, undiscriminating or unappreciative of the multiplicity of human values. This helps to explain how it is possible for people of divergent religious traditions to respect and appreciate one another. For this also is one of the facts of life we ought to understand.

Now we come to valuations and proposals of valuations of a third type, which have already been introduced briefly. These ascribe value to particular occasions or sets of occasions of experience. We are concerned here with religious valuations of particular occasions of experience.

An appraisal of an occasion of experience may ascribe intrinsic value to the experience, saying it was or would be good to have that experience apart from any contribution its occurrence might make to other experiences or to a whole of life. Or it may ascribe contributory value to the experience, saying it was or would be good because it enhances the value of some other experience or of a whole of life. Or the occasion of experience may be valued in both ways.

A preliminary point is analogous to one made earlier: oppositions cannot occur between expressions of satisfactions found in occasions of experience; oppositions can occur between proposals of valuations of occasions of experience. Speakers in $S$ can recognise that as a matter of fact they find religious satisfactions in different occasions of experience, and that the satisfactions they find are different. To the extent that this is true it is simply a matter of fact.

But there can be oppositions between judgements about the value of having such experiences and hence between proposals of valuations of them. Reflecting on some satisfaction found or anticipated, someone may decide that having the experience was or would be intrinsically good, leaving out as far as this judgement is concerned its connections with other occasions. Or, with or without an ascription of intrinsic value, he may judge that having the experience was or would be good by virtue of its contribution to something else. And in both of these cases opposed judgements are possible.

Suppose $B$ judges that some experience was or would be a good thing to have because it contributes to a certain envisaged whole of life which is good in itself. Then the elements of this complex judgement $(C)$ could be represented by a syllogism:

(i) The whole of life $W$ is good in itself.
(ii) The occasion of experience $e$ contributes to (enhances *or* is necessary for) $W$.
(iii) $e$ is (was, would be) a good experience to have.

Now negations of (iii) could occur by way of negations of (i) or by way of negations of (ii). First consider the former.

Suppose $B$'s and $\mathcal{J}$'s judgements about the values of wholes of life $W$ and $W'$ are in opposition, in the way we have seen above. $B$ thinks $W$ would be better than $W'$; $\mathcal{J}$ thinks the converse of this. Consequently their appraisals of the contributory values of particular occasions of experience may be opposed, though not necessarily so.

Thus $B$ is free to recognise that a prophet found a certain satisfaction in speaking for God on some occasion. Still, in view of the whole of life to which $B$ ascribes intrinsic value, his appraisal of the value of having the experience the prophet had could be opposed to the prophet's own appraisal of it. $B$ could say it was in some respect not a good thing to have that experience: 'it does not conduce to enlightenment' or 'it hinders enlightenment'. Conversely $J$ could recognise the satisfaction a Zen monk finds in satori, but say that having such experiences tends to make us unfit to do the will of God.

Here the dissenter in each case not only recognises that the other finds satisfaction in the experience; he could grant further that, given (i), (iii) would be true because (ii) is true. $J$ could grant that $e$ would indeed contribute to $W$. But he does not accept $B$'s valuation of $W$. He ascribes a lower value to it than to the whole of life he himself envisages. Or he may even ascribe a disvalue to it: 'it is a bad thing for people to live like that' or 'on the whole it is better that people should not live that way'. Hence their judgements of the contributory value of the occasion in question are opposed. One judges that the occasion contributes to the most satisfying whole of life; the other judges that it does not. So the disagreement about the complex judgement $C$ stems from a disagreement about (i).

But this is not the same as saying that a disagreement about (iii) must follow from a disagreement about (i). For $J$ could agree with $B$ that $e$ was a good experience to have but think it was good in some other way than $B$ says it is. For in $B$'s ascription of contributory value $(C)$ he is saying that $e$ is good *qua* its contribution to $W$. So, though $J$'s disagreement with (i) does not itself commit him to disagreement with (iii), since he may grant that $e$ was good in some other way – that it had some beneficial effect or other for example, he is still in disagreement with the complex value judgement $C$.

Ascriptions of contributory value to particular occasions of experience can be opposed in another way, stemming from disagreements about (ii). In these cases the dissenter holds that, even if (i) were true, (iii) is not true because (ii) is not true. $J$ may hold that $B$'s ascription of contributory value to $e$ on the ground of (i) is not warranted, because $e$ does not really enhance the value of $W$. $B$ has not rightly understood $e$ and hence is mistaken in his appraisal of its contributory value. Indeed $J$ may hold that a better analysis of $e$ would show that it would contribute to a different whole of life than that which $B$ envisages, that it would really contribute to $W'$ instead of to $W$.

Many religious arguments, especially dialectical arguments
82

(15), deal in oppositions of this sort. Speakers ask their opponents to rethink their experiences – perceptual experiences, experiences as children, parents, friends or citizens, in perplexity or sorrow or joy, with a view to showing that some experience does or does not contribute to a certain whole of life. Psychoanalysts ask their patients to rethink their experiences in a somewhat similar way, in this case with a view to seeing what whole of life the experiences could contribute to.

Finally oppositions between ascriptions of intrinsic value to particular occasions of experience are possible. *B* says that a certain occasion of experience was or would be a good thing, apart from any contributory values it might have; *J* says it was or would be bad for *B* or perhaps for anyone to have that experience, or experiences like that, leaving any contributory values out of consideration, or that having the experience was or would be worse than having some comparable experience.

Proposals of valuations of a fourth type should be mentioned briefly. All of the major religions involve communities which give each of them a social identity, though the institutional structures of these communities vary widely in their character and in their importance (16). Also doctrines of some of these religions propose valuations of the religious community itself as an enduring and changing social reality, for example of the Sangha, the people of Israel, or the Church.

Some doctrines ascribe intrinsic religious value to participation in the life of the community and thus inherent value to the community itself by virtue of its spiritual character. Consider 'How goodly are your tents, O Jacob, your dwelling places, O Israel' (Numbers 24:5) which begins the synagogue liturgy for morning prayer, and 'Blessed is concord in the Order; blessed is the austerity of those who live in concord' (*Dhammapada* 194, tr. Radhakrishnan). Doctrines to this effect are implicit in acts of adherence to the community such as 'I take refuge in the Sangha' and 'I believe in the holy Catholic Church'. Sometimes a community is valued for its contributions to the world. Some of these ascriptions of contributory value refer to immediate functions of the community, for example teaching the Dharma out of compassion for the world, bringing light to the nations, or preaching the gospel to all nations. Others occur in a wider framework of

83

world history, as in prophetic visions or in Augustine's 'City of God'.

Oppositions of these doctrines are clearly possible since the valuations which are being proposed depend on such primacy-ranking valuations as B2v and J2v and on valuations of the good life such as B3v and J3v. So if B2v and J2v or B3v and J3v are opposed, then doctrines proposing valuations of the Sangha and of the people Israel could be opposed. This does not imply that all the valuations of other communities by a member of one of them must be negative. Here as elsewhere there is room for recognition of the satisfactions found in the life of another community, for some of its moral achievements, and for some of its historical contributions to its world.

Now, summarising with a backward cast of our net, we have considered four points where those doctrines of different religions which have the force of proposing valuations could be opposed:

1. Proposals of valuations ascribing intrinsic value to the attainment of some end such as the attainment of Nirvana in B2v, or inherent value to some existent such as God in J2v. Valuations of this sort, ascribing a primacy in some category or an unrestricted primacy, seem to have key roles in schemes of religious doctrines.

2. Proposals of valuations of envisaged wholes of life as in B3v and J3v, ascribing either intrinsic or contributory value or both to these wholes of life.

3. Proposals of valuations ascribing intrinsic or contributory value to particular occasions or sets of occasions of experience.

4. Proposals of valuations of religious communities as historical realities.

In all these cases the doctrines are opposed if the valuations are incompatible. If the proposals of valuations are addressed to some particular person, and if that person cannot without absurdity make the valuations, the proposals are opposed. And if no one could make both valuations without involving himself in some absurdity, then the doctrines are opposed without restriction. Incompatibilities of valuations are more intimate and personal than incompatibilities of courses of action, and hence are a more direct threat to integrity of character. For some courses of action are incompatible by virtue of external circumstances

84

alone, whereas valuations are freer in respect of external circumstances. But the characters of human beings are not infinitely plastic, and there are limits on what is permitted by consistency of character. That is why no one can judge that something is good in a certain way and also bad in that way, or that something is better than and worse than another in a certain way, or that both of two things are best of all, without involving himself in that form of absurdity which consists in confusion about what he is.

Once more we should observe how much room is left for positive valuations of alien religions and their adherents, keeping in mind a simple but crucial distinction: an opposition of doctrines is not an opposition of persons. The sense of 'opposition' when we speak of oppositions of doctrines and its sense when we speak of oppositions of persons or communities are so different that they can be confused only by unconscious and unfortunate plays on the word. This distinction between doctrines and persons, between logic and morals, can itself be embedded in the doctrines of a religious tradition, and such doctrines could be found.

More particularly the following attitudes and judgements are not excluded by the presence of doctrines which propose incompatible religious valuations. Even if $M$ and $N$ hold opposed doctrines of this type, still $M$ can recognise and appreciate:

(i) aesthetic values of objects produced in $N$'s tradition – pieces of literature, buildings, sculptures, paintings, dramatic forms including ceremonies, and others;

(ii) moral virtues which are nurtured by $N$'s tradition and found in the lives of its adherents, such as honesty, seriousness, and charity;

(iii) intellectual virtues exhibited in the literature of $N$'s tradition and the discourse of its adherents, such as acuteness, clarity, rigour, power, and balance of judgement;

(iv) the satisfactions found by $N$, and other adherents to his tradition, in particular occasions of experience and in the wholes of life they envisage; and

(v) some of the historical contributions of $N$'s tradition to social life, in particular environments.

All this is possible if $M$ takes the trouble to learn something

85

about $N$'s tradition. Perhaps $M$'s curiosity about such matters would be reinforced by some of the teachings of his own tradition. Even so there are limits on anyone's capacity for sympathetic imagination and appreciation which he does well to recognise in formulating his judgements.

But even at best $M$'s judgements of all these sorts are likely to strike $N$ as more or less superficial and perhaps even patronising. He is likely to think that $M$ has missed the main point, and he is likely to be right if there were no more to it than this. What more might there be?

It would not be strange and certainly not impossible for two speakers in $S$ to find some religious valuations on which they were agreed or at least not opposed, along with the aesthetic, moral and other valuations I have just mentioned. For if some pair of doctrines of different religions, which propose valuations, are opposed it does not necessarily follow that all proposals of valuations which are doctrines of those religions are opposed. Oppositions at some points do not involve oppositions at all points. This is for two interconnected reasons: (i) the internal structures of doctrinal schemes are not rigidly or mechanically articulated but have a certain loose-jointedness; and (ii) between pairs of schemes, in some cases more than others, there is a certain logical distance marked by a shortage of interchangeable terms, as we found in the case of B1 and J1. This means also that doctrinal schemes are capable of development in response to new experiences and new conditions of existence, and it means further that the lines of development of doctrinal schemes might lead to unexpected convergences.

Still it remains true, we are supposing, that $M$ and $N$ hold opposed valuations and, supposing that these are central to the bodies of doctrine, one could well understand $N$'s reserve if their opposition is obscured by $M$'s enthusiasm for the aesthetic value of a Grandhara sculpture or a tea ceremony or a passage of Hebrew poetry, or for Gautama's force of mind or the moral earnestness of Amos. Truth must be kept in proportion, and candour on central issues is necessary to keep it so. Without this $N$'s unhappiness would be justified.

# 6   Proposals for Belief

We have been using the following pairs of sentences among others as working examples of religious doctrines, considering them as possible utterances in $S$:

B1   The Dharma is the path to attainment of Nirvana.
B2   Aim at attaining Nirvana.
B2v   Nirvana is the supreme goal of life.
B3   Live in accord with the Dharma.
B3v   The good life is a life in accord with the Dharma.
B4   Attainment of Nirvana is the only way of emancipation from suffering, which is intrinsic to conditioned existence.

J1   The Torah teaches us to respond rightly to God.
J2   Respond rightly to God.
J2v   God is holy.
J3   Live in accord with the Torah.
J3v   The good life is a life in accord with the Torah.
J4   God is our Lord and Maker, creator of heaven and earth and all that is in them, the judge of all nations and the fountain of life.

In this chapter we consider the force (in $S$) of assertions of B4 and J4 and other similar doctrines, and how such doctrines could be opposed to one another. We ought to begin by reviewing some differences between these assertions and assertions of some other types.

Some assertions have the force of informative utterances. These occur in situations where the speaker is supposed to be in a position to know what is the case and the hearer is supposed not to be in a position to know what is the case. Hence the speaker

87

is in a position to tell the hearer what is the case. (The elders of the clan tell the youths about their primordial ancestors; a mathematics teacher tells his beginning class in trigonometry how the symbols are used; I tell my companion, who has no watch, what time it is; I tell my doctor that I have a pain in my back.) The speaker is acknowledged to be in a position of authority with respect to the subject of the utterance.

Assertions of B4 and J4 cannot have this force in $S$. Speakers in $S$ can indeed be informative when they define or explain doctrines of their traditions, but not when they are asserting them. No speaker in $S$ could reasonably expect that his assertion of a doctrine of his religion would be taken as an informative utterance.

Though valuations are built into B4 and J4 the main point in asserting them is different from the point in asserting B2v/J2v and B3v/J3v. The main point in asserting B4 and J4 is to speak to an interest in knowing what is the case, knowing what existents there are and what the conditions of existence are. In this respect they are like informative utterances. But since in $S$ the speaker is not conceded authority in these matters, these assertions have the force not of informative utterances but of proposals for belief.

So in utterances of B4 and J4, and expansions and developments of them, the speaker puts forward an account of what is the case for belief by his hearers. He thus claims that what he says is true. Ordinarily he is reasonably sure that what he says is true. He may even think there is a valid and conclusive argument for the doctrine and hence may claim to know it is true in a very strong sense of 'know'. Still, the situation $S$ being what it is, his assertion has the force of a proposal for belief, not that of an informative utterance. The situation does not commit his hearers to taking what he says as true. Just as he is not in a position to command his hearers, to tell them what to do, he is not in a position to tell them what is the case. What the situation permits is to recommend courses of action and to propose beliefs.

The most natural way to make the proposals of valuations we studied in the last chapter is to put them as assertions. What is the force of these assertions? Certainly they do not have the force of informative utterances, though in the course of

88

supporting them informative utterances, about the speaker's experiences for example, are in order if they are relevant. But they do not have the same force as proposals for belief either. It is one thing to propose that something is the case, that there is such and such an existent or that some condition of existence holds. It is another matter to propose that some actual or possible existent or state of affairs be valued in a certain way. Different sorts of judgements are being called for.

Emotivists, in ethical theory, seem to put the difference as follows: proposals for belief make truth-claims; proposals of valuations do not. If we say this we seem to imply that valuations are either arbitrary preferences or emotive reactions. But this does not do justice to the way valuations actually work in discourse. So I believe it is better to say that assertions of both sorts make truth-claims, and that different though overlapping sets of principles of judgement are called for. Judgements that existents are good or bad in certain ways have to be made in accord with a wider range of norms of judgement than the range of norms required for judgements about what existents there are and what the conditions of existence are, because saying that something is good or bad in a certain way is saying more than saying it does or does not exist. But the argument of the last chapter does not hang on this question. Just as course-of-action recommendations can be opposed even though their main point is not to make truth-claims, so proposals of valuations can be opposed whether or not their main point is to make truth-claims.

Another way of getting a perspective on proposals for belief in $S$ is to review their connections with course-of-action recommendations and with proposals of valuations. This will help to show how beliefs, along with courses of action and valuations, are constituents of the patterns of life which the speakers in $S$ are engaged in recommending.

A course-of-action recommendation is acceptable without absurdity only if the course of action can be carried out. So the recommendation contextually implies that the course of action can be carried out and thus that certain existential conditions hold – physical states of affairs, facts about the constitutions and characters of certain human beings, and some general conditions of existence. If the relevant existential conditions do not hold, then the speaker is recommending something which is in fact impossible and thus committing an absurdity. So one way proposals for belief like B4 and J4 will occur in $S$ is this: doctrines of this sort assert existential conditions on which the validity of course-of-action recommendations depends.

Proposals for belief are connected with valuations as well. We are construing valuations as judgements ascribing value of some kind (intrinsic, inherent, contributory) and in some mode (absolute, comparative, or relative to persons) to some actual or possible existent (object, occasion, state of affairs, whole of life). Beliefs are ingredient in these judgements in the following ways:

(a) If the valuation is an appraisal of some actual existent it involves a reference to that existent, and if anyone proposes the valuation he is responsible for explicating the reference, as we saw in the last chapter. Thus a proposal of some valuation of God implicitly proposes some beliefs or other about God, which the speaker should be willing to explain and develop and, if necessary, to support by argument. So some proposals for belief in $S$ will occur by way of explaining and supporting references to logical subjects of valuations.

(b) If the valuation is an appraisal of a possible existent – some object which might come into existence or some possible occasion of experience or state of affairs, then the real possibility of the existent depends on some set of existential conditions which are believed to hold. Thus a proposal that attainment of Nirvana be valued as the supreme goal of life would depend for its validity on a supposition that attainment of Nirvana is a real possibility. And if anyone proposes this valuation he is responsible for explaining and if necessary arguing for some existential conditions which make attainment of Nirvana a real possibility, for instance that conditioned origination (*pratitya-samutpada*) is a general fact about existence and that strict determinism is not true (1). So the functions of some proposals of belief in $S$ will be to assert and to argue that certain conditions hold, on which proposals of valuations of possible existents depend for their validity.

It follows that proposals of valuations of these sorts in $S$ carry with them implicit proposals for belief. This puts us in a position to do rough justice, which is all they deserve, to disputes about whether religious judgements are 'subjective' or 'objective'. A good starting-point for putting the question into manageable form would be to say that religious judgements involve valuations, and that these valuations involve references to existents and suppositions of existential conditions.

These interconnections help to show that while the primary point of some religious doctrines is to recommend courses of actions, the primary point of others is to propose valuations, and the primary point of yet others is to propose beliefs, doctrines of these different sorts can enter into a more or less coherent pattern in the doctrinal scheme of some religion. And as a generalisation this seems to hold true of the major religions. For their doctrinal schemes generally reflect strong interests in relating courses of actions and valuations to the way things are.

The patterns of life which are taught in the major religions are likely to call for assertions of beliefs at various points. For example, in many liturgical situations, such as saying the Shema or the Apostles' Creed or the *shahāda* or delivering sermons and other addresses, speakers are often expected to give their utterances the force of deliberate assertions, to be mindful of what they say and to mean what they say, avoiding 'vain repetitions'. Again, assertions of beliefs have a place in the teaching activities of a religious community, in the education of the young and of converts and in continuing the education of those brought up in the faith. Furthermore, it seems reasonable to suppose that if anyone has adopted some way of life wholeheartedly he will have something to say in situations which are not shaped and controlled by his own community. And in these situations it is even more likely that explaining his way of life will call for assertions of beliefs.

Still a rider needs to be added, since it is not the business of critical philosophy of religion to say how the doctrines of any particular religion should be developed. If some religious community, in the course of developing its doctrines, should come to the point of renouncing beliefs as constituents of its way of life, the situation would be problematical in the following way. That community would have to interpret its doctrines as purely directive or purely expressive or as combining these two functions without any admixture of assertions. And, in explanation of this policy, it would have to show that those doctrines which

91

recommend courses of action have no existential suppositions, and that those doctrines which express valuations have no references. This might not be easy. One practical consequence might be that none of its adherents would participate in $S$.

How then could doctrines of different religions be opposed if they are proposals for belief? The meaning of opposition is relatively unproblematical in this case, but it should be connected up with the other types of oppositions we have discussed. Then the case of B4 and J4, which we take as a working example, will need a good deal of attention.

In general doctrines are opposed if they cannot be accepted jointly without absurdity. Thus course-of-action recommendations are opposed if, for example, it is physically impossible to carry out both. For accepting these doctrines means undertaking to carry out the courses of action. Proposals of valuations are opposed if the valuations cannot be made jointly without absurdity, if for example one doctrine says a certain existent is good in a certain way and another doctrine says it is bad in that same way, or if a primacy-ranking predicate is asserted of different logical subjects. For accepting these doctrines means making the valuations.

Similarly, doctrines proposing beliefs are opposed if they cannot be accepted jointly without absurdity. Even if we should not wish to say that what is asserted in a proposal of a valuation is a proposition, we have no inhibitions against saying that what is asserted in a proposal for belief or in an informative utterance is a proposition (except general inhibitions if any against speaking of propositions as well as of sentences and sentence-utterances). So here the standard rules of alethic logic clearly apply. But this can be put without speaking of propositions, as follows. Where we have an utterance of a doctrine in which a proposal for belief (or, I would add, a proposal of a valuation) is being made, to accept the doctrine is to take what is said in the utterance as true. Where we have utterances of different doctrines in which proposals for belief are being made, to accept the doctrines is to take what is said in each of the utterances as true. But if what is said in one and what is said in the other cannot both be true, then both what is said in one and what is said in the other cannot be taken as true without absurdity. Hence the doctrines cannot be

92

accepted jointly without absurdity and so are opposed. Probably we all commit many such absurdities without knowing that we do. Happily the practical consequences are often trivial; unhappily sometimes they are not.

Knowing what it means to say that proposals for belief are opposed does not tell us which ones are opposed and in particular whether B4 and J4 are opposed. For no oppositions lie on the surface of the sentences. For instance J4 does not explicitly say or obviously imply that suffering is not intrinsic to conditioned existence, and B4 does not clearly deny that there is a creator of the world. In $S$ it might be natural to suspect some underlying oppositions here, especially if oppositions had resulted from developments of B1–3 and J1–3. But whether B4 and J4 are in fact opposed would depend on how these doctrines are developed by the speakers. And since in $S$ the speakers are advancing doctrines of their religions, this would depend on what developments their traditions permit. Again, we can only look for some possible though hopefully not unplausible developments.

One very natural place to start is with doctrines about God, for references to God are prominent in J-doctrines and we are likely to expect oppositions between J-doctrines about the existence and nature of God and some B-doctrines or other. But this is not as easy as one might think. Consider for example:

B4a  There are no supernatural beings.
J4a  There is a supernatural being.

Though this is clearly an opposition, indeed a contradiction, does it give us an opposition of religious doctrines and in particular does it give us an opposition derived from B4 and J4? It might indeed formulate an opposition between an adherent of some religion and a religious or non-religious sceptic, supposing that the somewhat shaky concept of a supernatural being could be firmed up reasonably well in some way or other. But we are looking for ways in which doctrines of different religions could be opposed.

In Buddhist scriptures there are many, many *devas* and other non-worldly beings who play various parts in the life of the universe. But let us suppose for the sake of the argument that Buddhist doctrines came to be developed in a modernist way,

93

looking on the tales of the *devas*, including Mara the evil one, as mythological, so that it might be permissible for some Buddhist to assert B4a. Still one would wish to know what religious interest would be attached to this assertion, and more particularly whether there is some connection between B4 and B4a. In other words, is B4a a genuine development of B4? For not everything that an adherent of some religion is permitted by his tradition to assert is thereby a doctrine of that religion.

Also the relation of J4a to J4 has to be considered. If J4a means, 'There is at least one supernatural being and perhaps more', then though it might be admitted as an implication of J4 – provided again that 'supernatural being' could be given some clear meaning, it would seem too trivial an inference to have the force of a religious doctrine. What is more to the point, it would be seriously misleading in a monotheistic tradition.

One might well feel that the contrast B4a/J4a fails to catch the force of B4/J4 therefore, and that it fails to express a genuine engagement between them.

Similarly with:

B4b    There are many supernatural beings.
J4b    There is only one supernatural being.

Again, apart from the shakiness of the concept of a supernatural being, one would have to ask whether this captures part of the force of B4 and J4. For traditional Judaism admitted angels, demons and Satan. But even if *J* could deny B4b, regarding these stories as myths in the same way *B* might assert B4a, these formulations do not seem to bring out the underlying issue.

But perhaps they come closer to capturing part of the issue between B4 and J4 than B4a and J4a do, and the reason for this is interesting. The obvious point is that J4b reflects the traditional stress of Judaism on monotheism. But the form of J4b has a more general significance also. In 'The Questions of King Milinda' there is a discussion of why only one Arahat Buddha (Tâthagata) can arise in a world at one time. One reason that is given is as follows: if two Buddhas could appear at the same time, then all those passages [of scripture] where the Buddha is said to be the most excellent, the most exalted, the highest of all, the peerless one, without an equal, the matchless one, who hath

94

neither counterpart nor rival – all would be proved false' (SBE v. II, p. 50). This suggests how religious import gets attached to some propositions which say there is only one *x*, by way of valuational primacy-ranking predicates such as those we studied in B2v and J2v. At the same time, since J4b does not obviously express a valuation, it also brings out by way of contrast the poverty of J4b in religious import. J4 is not itself deficient in this way.

Clearly a better bet would be:

B4c   There is no creator of the world.
J4c   There is a creator of the world.

This is partly because J4c is clearly said in J4. But still there are complications. Refinements would have to be considered. A minor point is that *B*'s tradition might wish to insist there are many worlds, not just one. Also, does J4c commit the speaker to saying there was a time when the world was not? Or to saying that the creator is also the sole determinant of every event? Or that the action of the creator in the history of the world is utterly unaffected by the events in that history?

On the other hand does B4, or some development of B4, commit the speaker to an assertion of B4c? Here we have to consider not only whether *B*'s tradition permits him to assert B4c, though not making it a doctrine of the tradition, but whether the tradition rules out both assertions of B4c and assertions of J4c. In the Pali literature the Buddha teaches that certain questions should be set aside and left unanswered (2). Among these are whether the world is eternal, whether it is not eternal, whether it is finite, and whether it is infinite. One reason for setting aside these questions is as follows: 'These (questions) are not connected with the goal, with the teaching nor with the fundamentals of the religious life and do not conduce to disinterest, dispassion, cessation, tranquillity, higher consciousness (v.l. higher knowledge), realisation and Nirvāna' (3).

Now one might wonder whether, if the Buddha's teaching sets aside questions about whether the world is or is not eternal and whether it is finite or infinite, it does not thereby set aside questions about whether there is a creator or not. But perhaps we might leave open the conceptual possibility at least of a doctrine of creation which does not depend on the particular theses which

95

the Buddha here sets aside. If so, setting aside these theses would not entail setting aside both B4c and J4c. Also we shall see, later on, how the issue might have a more than speculative import, so that the Buddha's reason for setting aside the other questions would not apply to this one.

Historically it is reasonably clear that Buddhists have asserted B4c in the past. Hence there is some good evidence that the Buddhist scheme of doctrines and the Judaic scheme of doctrines are opposed at this point. But the Buddha's teaching about the *avyakata* questions can be instructive in the following way.

We should not expect the doctrines of different religions to match up at all points. In some cases this is due to diverse historical environments and in this sense is somewhat accidental. Certain problems happen to have been posed for one religion and not for another; for example, the problems Greek philosophy and later on medieval European civilisation posed for Christian theology were different from the problems Indian philosophy (and later on Chinese civilisation) posed for the development of Buddhist doctrines. But in other cases there are more internal reasons why matching doctrines are absent.

Confronted with some doctrine, a proponent of a different religion may have to say that his tradition inhibits him from any pronouncements one way or the other on the issue with which that doctrine deals. The issue itself springs from an interest which conflicts with the central concerns of his own tradition. A religious tradition can refuse to accept and teach some doctrine without embodying a denial of that doctrine in its own teachings. It can refuse to teach either the one or the other.

Certainly J4 says a great deal more than J4c and especially so if we should think of J4c as just a way of explaining the world. Also we have not connected up B4c with B4. So let us see whether we can capture more of the issue we sense between B4 and J4 by trying out some other formulations.

Suppose B4 should be developed in the following way: Conditioned existents are the only existents there are. All of the things we encounter in experience, and even we ourselves, are transient combinations of aggregates. These combinations originate when certain conditions occur and pass away when certain other conditions occur. So both our ordinary joys and our ordinary

96

sorrows, which arise from these combinations of aggregates, are themselves transient and impermanent and thus are themselves in a deeper sense sorrow-making.

Developed in this way the point of B4 is not just to say that no one can avoid having spells of suffering. Few if any would wish to deny that – certainly not $J$ – and it would hardly be worth saying. Instead, the point of B4 would be that suffering is intrinsic to conditioned existence in a far stronger sense. Walpola Rahula comments as follows on the first Noble Truth, about *dukkha*, which is ordinarily translated 'suffering':

> The Buddha does not deny happiness in life when he says there is suffering. . . . In the 'Anguttara-nikāya' . . . there is a list of happinesses (*sukhāni*), such as the happiness of family life and the happiness of the life of a recluse, the happiness of sense pleasures and the happiness of renunciation, the happiness of attachment and the happiness of detachment, physical happiness and mental happiness, etc. But all these are included in *dukkha*. Even the very pure spiritual states . . . attained by the practice of higher meditation, free from even a shadow of suffering in the accepted sense of the word . . . are included in *dukkha* (4).

This development not only adds force to saying that suffering is intrinsic to conditioned existence in B4, it also helps to see how B4 supports the recommendation B2: Aim at attainment of Nirvana, and the valuation B2v: Nirvana is the supreme goal of life; thus it would bring us closer to the religious point of the utterance.

Now does this development of B4 imply that there is no actual existent of such a character that, by relation to it, life can include in Whitehead's phrase 'a mode of satisfaction deeper than joy or sorrow'? (5) If so perhaps we could formulate an opposition between B4 and J4 by way of:

B4d    There is no actual existent of such a character that, by relation to it, life can include a mode of satisfaction deeper than joy or sorrow.

J4d    There is an actual existent of such a character that, by relation to it, life can include a mode of satisfaction deeper than joy or sorrow.

It is not hard to see how J4d could be a development of J4, with the metaphor 'the fountain of life' particularly in mind. Of course J4 says much more than this, but our problem is not to give a full and systematic rendering of the meaning of J4. It is only to find some part of J4's meaning, some implication of J4, which would be useful for formulating a possible opposition with some development of B4.

It is not so clear how B4 could imply B4d, but we have already made a start with the discussion above about the deeper root of suffering. That could be connected up with B4d in the following way. The deeper root of suffering lies in our thirst or craving for sense-pleasures and more generally for existence and becoming. This thirst arises from ignorance, from failure to see that all the things to which our cravings are attached are transient and impermanent. All existent things are transient combinations of aggregates, including ourselves; there is no permanent soul or self or ātman. So, it might seem, recognition of the truth of B4d is crucial for understanding the truth of B4 and for embarking on the raft (the Dharma) which carries us to the farther shore, Nirvana. In this way, it seems, B4 might be developed so as to imply B4d.

However, though B4d/J4d may have a certain initial plausibility as an opposition of doctrines of different religions, it is very likely that the speakers in $S$ would have to explore this matter much further in the course of their conversation. One problem is that the term 'actual existent' has a philosophical flavour and brings with it reminiscences of disputes in the Western philosophical tradition about what sorts of things there are, and of various ontologies in which this question has been treated. We might put to one side the possibility that $B$ may not be well acquainted with the ontological options in the Western tradition. For our purpose we could stipulate that he is, under condition 2 of $S$. The more serious matter is whether the traditions of $B$ and of $J$ would countenance the use of such terms in formulations of their doctrines.

That is a matter for a religious tradition to make up its own mind about. There do not seem to be any *a priori* rules which would prohibit religious traditions generally from incorporating alien terms into their doctrinal schemes. Beyond that a word or

98

two can be said in support of our own procedure. When one sets out to study oppositions of doctrines of different religions in a philosophical way the most interesting cases are the difficult ones like our own problematical case, and what makes them difficult is a scarcity of common concepts. In these cases the only way one can proceed is to try out terms which may be alien to one or both of the doctrinal schemes which are being compared. This is a hypothetical and in that sense artificial way of going about the matter. But in doing so we are not out of touch with the historical realities. For it is a commonplace of the history of religion that doctrinal schemes have often absorbed alien terms into their structures. Christianity's inheritance from Judaism and from Greek philosophy, and Buddhism's inheritance from Hinduism, Jainism and otherwise from Indian philosophy, are only two striking cases in point. Of course the process of absorption trans-forms the alien concept and naturalises it, so to speak, within the developing tradition, and the process of naturalisation is con-trolled by the consistency-rules of the tradition even though these too may undergo development.

So we should not think of the doctrinal systems of different religions as necessarily static, for religions develop in the course of their histories, more slowly in some periods and more rapidly in other periods, and along with their development as social realities their schemes of doctrines develop also. Nor should we think of them as permanently sealed off from one another, for sometimes the shocks of contact with alien systems affect not only their social structures but also the development of their doctrines.

Still one cannot assume that a particular tradition will wel-come and absorb a particular alien concept. Hence our own procedure remains hypothetical and we should explore some of the possible resistances in $B$'s tradition and in $J$'s tradition to accepting B4d and J4d as formulations of doctrines.

One line of exploration of this matter in $S$ could begin with Plato's linking of actuality and power in the 'Sophist' (247E). An actual existent, one might say, without otherwise restricting the sense of the term, makes some difference in the characters of other existents and in the conditions of existence. From this starting-point it would still be fairly clear how J4b might be accepted as a partial explication of J4. But what about B4d? We might suppose that *B* would not wish to say that there are no actual existents at all, in this sense of the phrase, since the notion of *karma* (action) plays an important part in his scheme. But would this explanation of 'actual existent' lead to second thoughts about B4d? The conversation would have to canvass the domain of *B*'s ontology, to see whether it includes anything which would count against B4d under this explanation.

At first sight it seems obvious that Nirvana would not be described as an actual existent in this sense, though the arahat who has attained Nirvana is an existent who is by no means devoid of power. The gods bow down before him. The description of Nâgasena in 'The Questions of King Milinda', book I 40, conveys a sense of *numinous* power indeed. But sometimes Nirvana is said to be 'Ultimate Reality'. How is this to be taken? Is it a proposal of a valuation like some of those considered in the last chapter, with a uniquely-applying valuational predicate? Or is it also a proposal for belief about an actual existent, though of course a highly transcendent one, which by its existence makes a difference in the conditions of existence? At this point the complexities of Mahayana metaphysics would have to be taken into account.

Is the Buddha himself an actual existent by relation to whom, in the formula of B4d/J4d, life can include a mode of satisfaction deeper than joy or sorrow? Here again not only the testimonies of the early disciples but also the later developments of Amida doctrines and of esoteric doctrines would have to be explored, taking account of Buddhist art as well as of Buddhist philosophy as evidence. Does the concept of the Buddha-nature in all sentient beings count against taking B4d as a doctrine of the tradition? On a more abstract plane what do we make of the teaching of the Yogācāra school that Mind constructs the phenomenal world, especially if this is understood as a 'soteriological device'? (6) What is its soteriological significance?

If, contrary to B4d, there should turn out to be some B-doctrine about the Buddha Shakyamuni or about Amitabha or the Buddha-nature in all sentient beings or Mind or Absolute Nothingness or the True Self (7), which implied J4d, then one would have to study this doctrine and lay it alongside some comparable J-
100

doctrine to see what oppositions if any could be derived from *them.*

Our business is not to settle these questions about B4d, which would have to be decided if at all by reference to the history and literature of Buddhism and ultimately by the living tradition itself. It is not our business to say whether the Mādhyamika school represents the central tradition of Mahayana Buddhism – much less whether it represents the central tradition of Buddhism – or whether the Yogācāra school does. Nor is it our business to say whether the doctrines of some religion are more authentically formulated in the terms of some philosophical school or other than if they are formulated in some other manner. At the end of his exposition of the Mādhyamika system T. R. V. Murti adds 'a note of warning. It is possible, in our enthusiasm, to over-rate the part played by scholarship and the theoretical understanding of things in the task of regeneration' (8).

I have raised those questions about B4d only to exhibit a difficulty about formulating oppositions between doctrines of different religions, and to suggest how we would have to proceed in problematical cases. When the doctrinal schemes are deficient in common concepts one has to introduce concepts from other contexts, as we have been doing, to see whether at some point or other the disparate schemes can be brought to a common focus. In this way one's intuition of an underlying issue between them might or might not be borne out. *B* might refuse to grant that B4 implies B4d, and *J* might refuse to grant that J4 implies J4d. Going further back, *B* and *J* might find B4 and J4 unacceptable as formulations of doctrines of their traditions.

In that case one tries again, reformulating and refining possible oppositions, so long as the intuition of a hidden conflict persists. If not in one way, then perhaps in another. Now suppose these efforts fail and continue to fail. This may dissipate the intuition of an underlying opposition, though we may have learned a good deal in the process. Conceivably after a number of failures one might conclude there are no conflicting proposals for belief; that the doctrines of the two religions about existents and the conditions of existence are consistent with one another. But surely the possibilities ought to be explored first, and the object of this exercise is to show how that might be done.

101

But perhaps we have been too cautious about using the word 'God' in the formulations above. There may be occasions in $S$ where the concept of God has become reasonably clear, clear enough to make the following significant:

J4e    God exists.
B4e    God does not exist.

$B$ could argue for example that just as the idea of a permanent self is false and empty so is the idea of God. Both are projections of our ignorance and our desire for security. The truth is that just as we ourselves are composed of transient aggregates so also is the world, and only if we realise this can we win victory over our illusions and attain the peace of Nirvana. Supposing $J$ has a philosophical turn of mind he might argue in return that it is precisely the compositions of the aggregates and the relativity of finite events that we need a concept of God to understand. Or he might support J4e in other ways, some of them less speculative than this may sound.

Other issues might be explored, for example doctrines about the nature of a human person or about the structure of the physical world. Instead let us consider doctrines about the historical process, narrowing this down to the course of human events on this earth.

Many of us are likely to suppose that Buddhism and Judaism have very different and even incompatible doctrines about the course of human events on this earth. It is often said that Buddhist doctrines negate the historical process and that Judaic doctrines affirm it. We are struck by the prominence of certain large-scale historical events in the biblical narratives, for example the exodus, and by how the Jewish community has oriented itself to those past events and to a Messianic age in the future, giving these events a deep religious import. The liturgy, for example the Haggadah of Passover, enforces this impression strongly. One might imagine that this orientation to historical events is echoed in the phrase 'the judge of all nations' in J4. In contrast we are inclined to think of Buddhists as less historically minded or even as looking on the historical process as something to be escaped from, as B4 may suggest.

It does not take long to discover that, though there may be
102

some truth in these impressions, it is not simple and easy to formulate oppositions of B-doctrines and J-doctrines about the historical process, especially if we are looking for oppositions of beliefs. For many of the striking contrasts with which we begin turn out to be contrasts of valuations of historical events, not contrasts of assertions about how the historical process actually goes. It is assertions of the latter sort which would fall under the heading of proposals for belief. Can we formulate oppositions between B-doctrines and J-doctrines of this sort?

We would do well to put aside certain speculative doctrines, which would be consistent with any course which human events on this earth might take, for example doctrines saying that time is finite or infinite, and doctrines asserting determinism or in-determinism. Cosmological doctrines are too sweeping for our purpose. Likewise the following would not be directly helpful:

God acts in history.
All that happens is done by God.
God used Assyria as the rod of his anger.

For these would yield no foothold for oppositions of doctrines about the course of history, except oblique ones deriving from oppositions about God. Let us see whether there could be oppositions about history which are independent of those issues.

Consider the following:

B4f   The Buddha was enlightened (attained Nirvana) as he sat under the bo-tree.

J4f   Moses was given the Law on Mt Sinai.

If we take these as historical assertions they are consistent with one another, and it does not seem plausible that any other J-doctrine would be opposed to B4f or that any other B-doctrine would be opposed to J4f. Perhaps *J* might wish to redescribe the event referred to in B4f, so as not to commit himself to the possibility of attaining Nirvana as explained in other B-doctrines. But his doctrines might permit him to agree that an event which *B* would describe as in B4f actually occurred. Likewise *B* might wish to avoid committing himself to belief in the existence of God, yet he might have no doctrinal interest in denying that an event describable as in J4e actually occurred. We noticed in

103

Chapter 3 the curious fact that only rarely does a doctrine of one religion, to the effect that some particular historical event occurred, come into opposition with a doctrine of some other religion. Certainly it seems unlikely that any of $J$'s doctrines imply that the Buddha never existed or that he was not enlightened, and also unlikely that any of $B$'s doctrines imply that Moses never existed or even that he did not bring down tables of stone from Mt Sinai. Of course $B$ and $J$ might have their own opinions about whether such events occurred or not, but this is not the issue. The issue is whether oppositions of historical assertions are embedded in the doctrinal schemes of the religions to which $B$ and $J$ adhere.

In contrast, consider:

B4fv   Knowing that Buddha was enlightened under the bo-tree contributes to attainment of Nirvana.

J4fv   Knowing that Moses was given the law on Mt Sinai contributes to responding rightly to God.

B4fv might be explained as follows. The Buddha's authority as a teacher comes from his enlightenment. So his teachings, the Dharma, can be relied on as the path to Nirvana because he himself knew what it meant to be enlightened and how one comes to be enlightened. Also, it might be argued, one can hope to be enlightened oneself because one knows that Shakyamuni was enlightened. Or, one's hope of attainment of Nirvana is strengthened by knowing that it was attained by Shakyamuni. If no man were known to have attained it, could any man hope for it or (the weaker thesis) could he have such a lively hope?

Analogously for J4fv, responding rightly to God involves obeying his law, living in accord with the Torah as a God-given rule of life. But there must be some way of identifying his law, and we do so by reference to the event at Mt Sinai.

These are ascriptions of contributory value to those occasions of experience in which the historical events are apprehended. Apprehensions of the events are said to contribute to the intrinsic value of a whole of life which is oriented in a certain way, to attainment of Nirvana or to response to God. Thus from assertions that certain historical events occurred (B4f/J4f) we have developed valuations of those events, or rather valuations of knowing them. And by this development we seem to have taken

104

a step nearer to formulating an opposition. Indeed if B3v and J3v are opposed and if they are implicit in utterances of B4fv and J4fv in $S$, then the latter pair are obliquely opposed. But how could we develop a direct opposition?
Consider:

B4fvN   To live the good life it is necessary to know that the Buddha was enlightened under the bo-tree.

J4fvN   To live the good life it is necessary to know that the law was given to Moses on Mt Sinai.

Then $B$ might explain that the only exception to the necessity is the pratyeka-buddha, who attains enlightenment by himself. But since the pratyeka-buddha is 'as rare as the horn of a unicorn' and is indeed only an ideal type, since no one has ever been identified as a pratyeka-buddha, this not a real exception. And conceivably $J$ might add that J4fvN holds for non-Jews as well as for Jews (9).

Here again we would have an oblique opposition, if B3v and J3v are opposed. But this could be developed into a direct opposition by one additional step. Some doctrinal schemes include the concept of a body of knowledge which is *sufficient* for the good life (e.g., for righteousness or for salvation). Now suppose that either the B-scheme or the J-scheme includes this concept, or that both do. Suppose further, what seems highly plausible, that the B-scheme does not include knowledge of J4f, or that the J-scheme does not include knowledge of B4f, in the body of knowledge which is held to be sufficient for the good life, or that both of these hold. Then we would have derived a brace of direct oppositions from B4fvN/J4fvN. For if some body of knowledge is sufficient for $G$, and if this body of knowledge does not include $p$, then knowing $p$ is not necessary for $G$. With this additional development, $B$'s doctrines would lead him to deny J4fvN and $J$'s doctrines would lead him to deny B4fvN. The direct oppositions derived in this way can be exhibited as follows:

I B:   Knowledge of the Buddha's enlightenment is necessary for the good life.

  J:   Knowledge of the Buddha's enlightenment is not necessary for the good life.

105

II J: Knowledge of the giving of the law to Moses is necessary for the good life.
   B: Knowledge of the giving of the law to Moses is not necessary for the good life.

This assumes of course that B3v and J3v are opposed.

It is striking and a little curious that starting from B4f and J4f so much development was needed to arrive at oppositions of doctrines about history from these starting-points. And it is instructive that valuations played such an important part in this development. This reminds us again of the prominence of valuations in the structures of schemes of religious doctrines.

Some schemes of doctrines seem to value historical events more than others do, and one way to fund the common intuition that Judaism is a more historical religion than Buddhism would be to say that doctrines about historical events have a more important place in the Judaic scheme than they do in the Buddhist scheme, that J-doctrines value knowing historical events more than B-doctrines do. More historical events are valued, or, these events are valued more highly. This might be meant by saying that Judaism is more historically oriented than Buddhism. But such contrasts of valuations are not themselves oppositions, much less oppositions of beliefs.

But there might be oppositions of more general valuations of history in addition to the oppositions of valuations of particular historical events which we have discussed so far. Suppose some religion, for example Hinduism, had a doctrine ($d$) to the effect that there is no historical event such that knowing it is necessary for the good life (suppose it would be argued that the good life is a life oriented to attainment of *moksha*, or to realisation of the identity of the self and Brahman), or the far stronger doctrine ($d'$) that no bits of historical knowledge contribute to the good life. Then $d'$ would be in opposition both to B4fv and to J4fv, and $d$ would be opposed both to B4fvN and to J4fvN. So there could be oppositions of doctrines which assert general valuations of historical events.

We have been engaged in testing some common intuitions about religious doctrines which have to do with the historical process, the course of human events on this earth. Let us consider

106

now a pair of formulations, which have some plausibility as B- and J-doctrines, of assertions that events of a certain class do or do not occur in human history. These are clearly proposals for belief, but they introduce a different sort of issue than doctrines such as B4f and J4f, which assert the occurrences of single particular events, do.

B4g   Some human beings live more than once on this earth.

J4g   Every human being has only one life to live on this earth.

The former seems a clear inference from many utterances about rebirth which one finds in Buddhist literature, though certainly it is not a full statement of the doctrine of rebirth. Non-human beings are said to be reborn also, and there are various possible careers of existence. Further, there are nine possible abodes of being, of which the world of men is only one (10). J4g could plausibly be argued to be a Jewish doctrine, though the doctrine of transmigration of souls was highly developed in the Kabbalah, became a popular doctrine after 1550 (11), and in the eighteenth century was very generally accepted. But as elsewhere I do not want to claim that the formulations I use are true and faithful statements of doctrines of this or that religion. It is enough for our purpose if they are not obviously out of the running as candidates for being considered so.

These utterances are clearly opposed. Further, it seems very clear that these are not proposals of valuations but proposals for belief. The issue is whether or not events of a certain sort occur in the historical process which goes on on this earth. Doctrines of this sort clearly have to do with what existents there are and what the conditions of existence are.

At the same time one can see how these beliefs might be connected with the valuations of single events we were considering earlier. We can imagine that if someone accepted J4g he might be impressed with the decisiveness of a human being's life on earth. As far as what he wishes to do and be on this earth is concerned it is now in this life or never, though there may be later consequences. And we can imagine that this might encourage him to look upon certain particular historical events in a different

107

way than if he accepted B4g. This belief might influence his valuations of single historical events, and he might be more ready to attach decisive importance to some of them.

As our final example of doctrines about the historical process consider:

J4h  There will come a time when all nations will worship and obey God.

At the very outset this poses the problem: Is there some B-doctrine which might yield, by any sort of development, an opposition with J4h? That is the way this case will be instructive.

The problem is not whether B as an individual would disagree with the J-doctrine. This might well be true. But we are not interested in B's opinions as such but in the doctrines of his religion. We are studying the possibility of oppositions of doctrines of different religions.

J4h predicts a large-scale event in which the people of all nations will carry on activities describable as worshipping and obeying God. But this reference to God does not block out the possibility of a B-doctrine in opposition to J4h. For it would be possible to say that this event will or will not occur without supposing that God exists, or even if it were supposed that God does not exist. All that would be needed would be a doctrine which says or implies that no event describable in that way will occur. The question is: Are there any plausible candidates for B-doctrines which would have that effect?

In an important Mahayana sutra one finds the doctrine of the decline of the law (the Dharma). In the period beginning with the life of the Buddha the true law was taught. This period would be succeeded by a period in which distorted versions of the law would be taught. Then there would be a period in which the law would be neither heard nor taught nor even remembered. Then another Buddha would appear to begin another cycle. But this doctrine of the decline of the law would seem to yield no reason for denying J4h. Indeed one can imagine a Buddhist saying that if J4h should come true this would constitute clear evidence of the decline of the law!

Since I have not been able to think of any way to formulate a B-doctrine which might appear here as B4h, from which an

108

opposition to J4h might be developed, I shall leave the puzzle to scholars in Buddhist studies. But there is no general reason why some doctrine of one religion must always have a corresponding opposite among the doctrines of some other religion, and it may be that this is a case in point.

# 7 Some Concluding Reflections

Some religious doctrines recommend courses of action: inward or overt, ritual or moral, by oneself alone or together with others. That is to say, an utterance of the doctrine in standard conditions has the force of recommending to someone that he undertake the course of action. Other doctrines propose valuations; others again propose beliefs. In the major religions of the world, doctrines of these types are interconnected and organised, more or less, in their schemes of doctrines.

So when a religious community teaches its doctrines to its members it is teaching them a certain pattern of life in which courses of action, valuations and beliefs are ingredients. It does this not just by enunciating and presenting verbal formulations of the doctrines but by creating conditions which nurture that way of life.

It is different when, as sometimes it happens, doctrines of a religion are proposed to non-members of the community, sometimes indeed to members of other religious communities with doctrinal schemes of their own. In these cases doctrines have to be presented more on their own merits, as it were, without the antecedent support of those common habits of thought and action which hold within a religious community. Though often the difference is a matter of degree, especially in a modern pluralistic society where religious communities cannot be insulated easily from one another and from the world around them. The model situation $S$, the framework of this study, is of this latter sort: speakers who adhere to different religious traditions are recommending to one another the patterns of life taught by their traditions. It is the kind of situation in which oppositions of doctrines of different religions might occur concretely, not just as abstract possibilities.

Recommendations of patterns of life are opposed if some of

their constituents (course-of-action recommendations, proposals of valuations, proposals for belief) are opposed, that is to say if the courses of action, valuations and beliefs which belong to the patterns of life are incompatible. We have studied some of the ways these oppositions might occur and we have seen how our intuitions about them might be tested, how we could flush suspected oppositions from their coverts, if indeed they are there.

We can add some depth of perspective to our results by reflecting briefly on a theory about religions which depreciates oppositions of doctrines, and on some moral considerations which bear on $S$.

Consider the theory that all the major religions really say the same thing and hence their doctrines cannot really be opposed. Let us ask what this would mean if it is said of some pair of religions and how the question, if it is indeed a good question, could be decided in that case. For saying that all the religions really say the same thing would be equivalent to saying that this is true for every pair of religions, and it would have to be settled by taking them pair by pair. So let us suppose some speaker $H$ who says that religions $R^1$ and $R^2$ really say the same thing. Let us allow that $H$ may adhere to $R^1$ or to $R^2$ or to neither one, though perhaps to some third religion $R^3$.

Let us allow $H$ to make his claim more plausible, though at the same time more problematical, by restricting it to the 'essential' doctrines of $R^1$ and $R^2$. This would make it somewhat more plausible because now $H$ would not have to show that every pair of comparable doctrines in the two schemes really say the same thing. At the same time it would make his claim more problematical since he is now claiming to know which doctrines of $R^1$ are essential doctrines and which are not, and the same for $R^2$. First consider this latter point.

One rule for discriminating between essential and non-essential doctrines of $R^1$ would be as follows: Discover the norms of judgement which hold within $R^1$ on this matter and abide by them. For every religious community sooner or later develops norms of its own for judging which doctrines are more important than others, out of practical necessity. With this rule $H$ would accept the testimony of $R^1$'s scriptures as to what is essential, together

111

with the judgements of proponents of $R^1$ who are well educated in its tradition and well respected in the community, and the same for $R^2$. He could also appeal to widespread ritual and moral practices as evidence of what the community takes to be essential or not.

The alternative is to import norms of judgement from elsewhere. This is often done by external friends as well as external opponents of a religion. Thus friendly Hindu interpreters of Buddhism, for example S. Radhakrishnan, minimise the importance of the *anatta* doctrine in Buddhism, and Marxist opponents of Christianity maximise the importance of otherworldly doctrines in the Christian tradition.

Though a religious community may learn a great deal about itself from external friends and opponents, it has to embody what it learns in its own judgements and these judgements have to be in accord with its own norms of judgement. While external judgements about what is and what is not a doctrine *of* $R^1$, or what are and what are not the essential doctrines of $R^1$, may be serious and honest and enlightened, still there is a sense in which the non-member's judgements on these matters cannot be as responsible as those of members *of* $R^1$, whose judgements should also be serious, honest and enlightened of course. The point is that the non-member is not in a position to make his judgements come true, so to speak, as the member is. He is not in a position to shape the practice of the community in accord with what he claims its doctrines are. For this reason a religion has the right to the final word, if there is one, about which of its doctrines are essential to it (or more important) and which are not. This is a different question of course from the question whether its doctrines are true.

Coming back to the main point, there are two versions of $H$'s claim that the essential doctrines of $R^1$ and $R^2$ say the same thing, depending on different senses of 'say the same thing'. There is a straightforward version and there is a symbolic version. The straightforward version is as follows. What is said in standard utterances of essential $R^1$-doctrines is equivalent to what is said in standard utterances of comparable $R^2$-doctrines. The image is that of a translation from one language into another. In a standard utterance of '*il pluie*' the same thing is said as in a standard utter-

112

ance of 'it is raining'. Analogously, utterances of $R^1$-doctrines and comparable $R^2$-doctrines say the same thing with different vocabularies and different rules of syntax.

This version of $H$'s claim is testable and therefore vulnerable. If a great many past or present speakers of the '$R^1$-language' or of the '$R^2$-language' do not accept the equivalence, and especially if well-educated and widely-respected proponents of the doctrines refuse the equivalence, this would be a weighty objection to $H$'s claim.

It is not so clear whether the symbolic version of $H$'s claim is testable. It says that though two doctrines do not say the same thing straightforwardly they are both symbolic of the same thing. They point to the same thing though they do not say the same thing outright. For example W. T. Stace says:

> I shall maintain that always and everywhere, in all the great religions, there is in fact only one destination, one experience, even – with some qualification – one path, but that is 'hinted at' by means of different 'myths and images' which constitute the differences between the religions. (1) [The phrases within quotation marks are taken by Stace from T. S. Eliot's 'The Cocktail Party'.]

So $H$ could grant that what is said in some doctrine of $R^1$ is not equivalent to what is said in doctrines of $R^2$. The doctrines might even be opposed, if we pay attention to what they say. But that does not matter for (i) the real point is not what is said but what is hinted at. And (ii) both doctrines hint at the same thing. Thus two different sorts of theses are involved in the symbolic version of $H$'s claim.

(i) There are theses about what is and what is not essential in the doctrinal schemes of $R^1$ and $R^2$. $H$ claims that what is essential in the $R^1$-scheme is its hints at something or other, and that what its doctrines say outright is not essential to what $R^1$ 'really says'. And he makes a similar claim about $R^2$. These are hermeneutic theses about the two doctrinal schemes.

Now suppose that the $R^1$-scheme itself includes a hermeneutic doctrine to the effect that what is essential in the scheme is its hints, without of course saying what is hinted at, for to say that would stultify the hermeneutic doctrine. And suppose the same

113

for $R^2$. Then $H$'s hermeneutic theses would be on reasonably safe ground so far. But suppose that one of the schemes lacks such a hermeneutic doctrine about itself, or that both do. Then $H$'s own theory would be vulnerable in the way we noticed earlier. He would lay himself open to the possibility that the $R^1$ community or the $R^2$ community will not agree that he has rightly stated the way its doctrines are meant.

(ii) In addition to these theses about the doctrinal schemes of $R^1$ and $R^2$, $H$ makes a further claim. He claims not only that the essential elements in their doctrinal schemes are their hints, not what they say outright, that their doctrines are really only myths and images. He claims also that one and the same thing, one destination, one experience and one path, is hinted at in both.

What is one to make of this symbolic version of $H$'s claim, and particularly of the thesis that the doctrinal schemes of $R^1$ and $R^2$ hint at or point to one and the same destination, experience and path? One feature of this claim seems fairly clear. Ordinarily it is not put forward as just a generalisation arrived at by studying the histories and the literatures and the ways of life of the major religions. This is signalled sometimes by the fact that some religions are taken to hint at the one destination, experience and path more strongly than others do. More generally it is signalled by the fact that the speaker is himself proposing and advocating the one destination, experience and path, which he claims is being hinted at in the doctrinal schemes of $R^1$ and $R^2$.

At this point it makes a difference whether $H$ is speaking as a member of $R^1$ (or of $R^2$) or not. If he is speaking as a member of $R^1$ then it would be natural for anyone to understand his theses as phases of a dialectical argument for $R^1$. Such an argument might run as follows: If the doctrines of $R^2$ are taken in a more or less straightforward way, they run into difficulties. They generate internal inconsistencies and paradoxes, or they come into conflict with perceptual experience, the teachings of modern science, or enlightened modern morality. Since these consequences are unacceptable, the doctrines must be taken as myths and images if they are to be acceptable at all. And, since the destination, experience and path which are pointed to by the myths and images of $R^1$ yield the only satisfactory interpretation of the myths and images of $R^2$, it must be that the myths and images of

114

$R^2$ are hinting at that destination, that experience and that path. What else could be meant?

If on the other hand $H$ is not speaking as a member of either $R^1$ or $R^2$ and yet is advocating the destination, experience and path which he claims is hinted at in both of their doctrinal schemes, then it seems that he is speaking as an adherent of some other religion $R^3$, perhaps even of a new religion in which case his utterances would have a prophetic sound.

In any case if $H$ is himself advocating a pattern of life, which he thinks the doctrines of the major religions hint at, he becomes in effect a speaker in $S$. Both his theses and the norms of judgements he appeals to would have to be supported by argument, including dialectical arguments like the one above about $R^2$, against objections by other speakers. And it seems clear that objections would be relevant at a number of points. There is plenty of room for oppositions between his proposals and those of other speakers.

Indeed, having in mind our study of B2/J2 in Chapters 4 and 5, it seems that Stace's characterisation of what is hinted at, as a 'destination', an 'experience' and a 'path', already opts for a pattern of life which is teleological and mystical. This becomes clearer from Stace's later developments of the theme. We have seen how J-doctrines might generate oppositions with doctrines of this type, holding that the good life is a life oriented in a different way.

I have put Stace's words into $H$'s mouth. But other versions of what is hinted at could be given. $H$ might speak in a Kantian way instead and say that the one true religion, of which the doctrines of the positive religions are symbolic, is to regard all our duties as divine commands. These different versions of $H$'s claim might themselves be in opposition.

The following passage from the writings of the famous thirteenth-century Zen Buddhist, Dogen, reminds us that the issue we have been discussing is by no means just a modern one:

> Those who are lax in their thinking are saying that the essence of Taoism, Confucianism and Buddhism is identical, that the difference is only that of the entrance into the Way, and also that the three are comparable to the three legs of a tripod.

115

Many Buddhist monks of the great Sung (dynasty) have quite often said this. If people say such things, Buddhism has already gone from them (2).

We have been considering the possibility that when $H$ claims that all religions really say the same thing he himself is advocating the pattern of life which he says they all teach, whether he is speaking as an adherent to $R^1$ or $R^2$ or some other religion $R^3$ or whether he is speaking prophetically of some religion not yet fully in existence. Then his claim takes on the aspect of a phase in a dialectical argument for adopting that pattern of life. What else could the religions be saying if what they say is to be acceptable? Very often this is the kind of context in which the claim is made. But we can imagine such a claim being made in quite a different context. We can imagine a speaker saying that all the religions teach the same pattern of life and adding that it would be a bad thing to adopt that pattern of life. Instead of claiming that they all point to the same truth he might be claiming that they all exhibit the same illusion.

The problem is that if we take the claim as just an empirical generalisation, an observation based on comparative studies of the literatures of the major religions, of their historical development, and of their current expressions of belief and practice, it seems implausible. It is clear enough that there are structural similarities running through all the major religions – each of them has rituals for example, and that there are analogies among their doctrines, sometimes even striking analogies. But adding up all the similarities and analogies we can find among them seems to leave us far short of the evidence needed to warrant the claim that they are saying the same thing. So we feel the need of some explanation of why the claim is made. There must be something more to it than just an empirical generalisation.

Consider the following line of thought which may throw some light on the matter and which, in any case, will lead us into some reflections on the ethics of $S$, some moral considerations which bear on religious disagreements.

(i) It is not unusual for us to find that we have respect or affection for people whose doctrines are different from our own and even, we think, opposed to our own. This fact may come to

116

intrigue us as we reflect on it and it may seem to us to call for some explanation or other. In most cases we are aware of some important agreements in beliefs, valuations and practical doctrines which we have with these people. Still we may be struck by a disparity we feel between the respect and affection we have for them, or which they seem to have for us, and the extent to which their doctrines and ours are compatible. The degree of overlapping of the doctrines seems insufficient to account for the respect and affection.

(ii) So we begin to think there must be more in common between these sets of doctrines than meets the eye. How could we explain the respect and affection if that were not so? Along with the agreements in doctrines of which we are aware, but which seem insufficient to explain the respect and affection between us, must there not be other points of doctrine which we really have in common, of which we are not aware? Perhaps these are really implicit in the manifest doctrines, some of which are opposed. There is a unity of doctrines which is hidden by the differences.

(iii) Since we place a high value on the respect and affection we have discovered, we are led to place a high value on the hidden doctrines on which we suppose we agree. If there were not these hidden agreements we could not really enjoy the respect and affection. It is then a short step to thinking that the hidden doctrines, on which we agree, are really more important than those manifest doctrines which seem to be opposed. And if we suppose that the hidden doctrines are somehow implicit in the manifest ones then it is another short step to thinking that when we affirm the manifest doctrines we are really affirming the hidden ones. These are what we really believe. And since the people for whom we have respect and affection must be doing this too, we are all really saying the same thing. So the oppositions between their doctrines and ours, which set us to reflecting in the first place, must be only apparent, not real.

One question this suggests is: Do we have to agree with people to have respect and affection for them, and is it possible to have respect and affection only to the extent that we agree with one another? Affection is not very careful about rules, though a steady affection surely has some necessary connection or other with respect. But if we think of respect in something like Kant's

117

sense the answer to the question is no. In that sense respect is a duty, something we owe any person whatever including ourselves, regardless of his position in life, the courses of action he is carrying out, his valuations and his beliefs, without implying any indifference about these whatever. We are free to disapprove of his actions and to disagree with his valuations and beliefs and to oppose them with candour and vigour. Indeed this may be called for by respect. But the fundamental duty to respect persons remains. Various religions have doctrines which enjoin and interpret some such duty in one way or another. It may be thought of as a response to 'that of God' in every man, or to the Buddha-nature in every sentient being, or perhaps in other ways.

So as far as this fundamental or unconditional respect for persons is concerned we do not have to agree with other people to respect them, and the degree of our respect does not have to be proportioned to the degree to which we are in agreement. So there is no need to look for hidden agreements for that reason.

Along with this fundamental respect for persons there is another and perhaps more common sense of respect in which respect for a person is conditioned on approval of his habits and actions. In this sense which we may speak of as moral respect, we tend to lose respect for someone if we discover he has done something shameful, for example, or if he exhibits extraordinary moral weakness. Now is agreement in doctrines, whether these are construed in a straightforward way or in a symbolic way, necessary for moral respect? Consider how one speaker in $S$ might lose respect for another, setting aside for this purpose condition 5 (that they speak with candour and treat one another with respect and charity). Suppose a speaker defends his doctrines with arguments which, we have reason to think, he knows to be fallacious, or employs other persuasive devices to secure acceptance of them including perhaps speaking in misleading and even untruthful ways. Or suppose he is domineering or oily or obsequious towards other speakers. In these cases other speakers would have a diminished moral respect for him though their fundamental respect would remain.

But in such cases the grounds for loss of respect are independent of the doctrines the speaker holds and advances. One speaker might lose respect for another on these grounds whether or not

118

their doctrines are opposed or consistent with one another, or even if in utterances of their doctrines they are in effect saying the same thing. Any speaker in $S$ might be guilty of such faults. So it seems that moral respect does not depend on agreement in doctrines; it depends only on estimates of moral dispositions and behaviour.

It is the same where intellectual virtues rather than moral virtues are concerned. Setting aside conditions 2, 3 and 4 of $S$ (that the speakers are reasonably well educated in their own traditions, that they know reasonably well the literatures and histories of the other religions, and that they are reasonably intelligent and acute), suppose some speaker proves unable to follow subtle arguments or that he is not sensible of distinctions or that he is ignorant of the alternatives to his doctrines or of important facts which bear on them. Then the respect of the other speakers would be diminished on the grounds of his lack of intellectual capacity and ability, though he might suffer not at all in their moral respect, and their fundamental respect for him as a person would not be affected. Again, any speaker in $S$ is liable to such faults, for these faults are independent of what the doctrines of their traditions happen to be. So intellectual respect for one another does not depend on agreement in doctrines.

Though postulates of hidden agreements are not necessary to account for the respect and affection which speakers in $S$ might have for one another, still there are plenty of good reasons to look for convergences of doctrines and agreements of doctrines in such situations as $S$. The most basic reason would be a conviction that the truth is open to all. 'We all know the nature of life and of the real, though only with exquisite care can we tell the truth about them' (3). The presence of some such conviction would add another dimension to conversations in $S$. The proposals and explanations of doctrines, and the arguments for them, could be viewed in the larger setting of a common inquiry. In this setting the discovery of an opposition of doctrines would not be a discovery of a dead end, though it would be a discovery of a real fact; it might be the discovery of an opportunity. It could teach us something about the care we have to use to tell the truth. Various religions might have doctrines which bear on this too.

Furthermore, if we know how to discover hidden oppositions of doctrines then we know how to find hidden agreements of doctrines as well, if they are there to be discovered. For if sometimes we have intuitions that doctrines of different religions are opposed, though it is not clear just how, it is also true that sometimes we have intuitions that doctrines of different religions are consistent with one another or convergent with one another or even that in effect they say the same thing, though it is not clear just how. The way to test these latter intuitions is like the way to test the former ones. In both kinds of cases we have to try out possible developments of the doctrines. We would have to find out whether the developments we construct would be counted as doctrines of the religions, and then we would have to see what their consequences turn out to be.

Tolerance is often advanced as a virtue for situations like $S$, but it is not very clear just what tolerance amounts to and how it would have applications in $S$. No doubt tolerance is a good thing on the whole; certainly it is better than intolerance. But if we are thinking of personal attitudes and not of political policies there are puzzles about tolerance which leave us wondering how much of a moral virtue it is. Perhaps intolerance is more of a vice than tolerance is a virtue. In any case one might wonder whether tolerance is a sufficient guide for behaviour in $S$.

Does tolerance depend on indifference to issues and persons? If so it seems that tolerant men would be out of place in $S$, since the speakers in $S$ adhere to religious traditions and recommend to other people the patterns of life which are taught in these traditions. This seems incompatible with indifference to issues and persons. Does tolerance depend on scepticism? Can one be tolerant only to the degree to which one is sceptical? If one holds a belief strongly one could not be tolerant of contrary beliefs? One could be perfectly tolerant only if one had no beliefs at all? If that is practically impossible then it seems tolerance would not be a perfectible virtue. In any case tolerant men would again be out of place in $S$ for the reason given above, since speakers in $S$ are not sceptical about their traditions though they need not be uncritical about them.

Does tolerance, by virtue of its historical association with the political concept of toleration, imply that, just as the sovereign

120

power in the state has the right to tolerate or not to tolerate some activity within its bounds, so also I have the right to tolerate or not to tolerate the opinions of others? When I am tolerant, am I like a gracious sovereign? I generously concede to you the right to have your own opinions and to say what you think?

Can we be content with a moral concept which is haunted by such ghosts as these? While we should not wish to say 'Be intolerant', is not something more than tolerance needed to guide behaviour in $S$? Other virtues are needed to banish these ghosts.

Charity, in the old sense, is a livelier and more full-blooded virtue and it has some applications to conversations and arguments, though unfortunately some ghosts hover about it too, which other virtues would be needed to dispel. For example, it suggests a sense of spiritual superiority which would be deadly to give-and-take in $S$. But there is much to be said for it. It suggests offering something to someone else, not being churlish and holding back knowledge or insights or practical wisdom gained from experience, if we happen to have any of these. It suggests a concern for other people as persons, which produces respect and militates against use of unsound arguments, against over-persuasion and against taking advantage of ignorance or of status. It suggests paying attention to what others say and doing justice to what they have said. It suggests not holding another's faults against him. All this would help to promote productive conversations in $S$. But like all moral virtues charity is only a qualifier of persons and actions. One way of putting the substance which, in $S$, it qualifies is by the phrase 'speaking the truth [as the speaker sees it of course] in charity'.

Presumably speakers in $S$ would find some principles in their own traditions to guide their behaviour in the conversation, if their traditions do not discourage or rule out such conversations. (If a tradition does rule out conversations in which a speaker is on an equal footing with proponents of other religions it would have no speaker in $S$.) And a comparative study of the principles of various religions which bear on behaviour in $S$, principles bearing on attitudes to other religions, on the conduct of arguments, and on behaviour when disagreements occur, would be of great interest. This is only one of a number of neglected topics in comparative ethics and in the comparative study of religions.

121

At the same time, if a conversation in $S$ is to go at all well some moral conditions or other have to be satisfied. If, that is to say, impasses due to defensiveness (arising from insecurity) and malice are to be prevented from frustrating the conversation. For many habits of thought and speech which would be appropriate in other kinds of situations would be counter-productive in $S$. Hence there is room for direct study of the moral requirements of such situations as well.

# Notes

## CHAPTER 1

1. See C. K. Ogden, 'Opposition, A Linguistic and Psychological Analysis' (Bloomington: Indiana University Press, 1967).

2. I have developed some principles of judgement which would be relevant to external oppositions of religious doctrines in 'Meaning and Truth in Religion' (Princeton University Press, 1964).

3. See the discussion between Professor Masao Abe, a Zen Buddhist philosopher, and various Christian theologians in 'Japanese Religions', vols. 3 and 4 (1963–1966), and Abe's review article on Tillich in 'The Eastern Buddhist', n.s., vol. ɪ (1965).

4. 'Judaism in the First Centuries of the Christian Era, The Age of the Tannaim' (Harvard University Press, 1927–30).

5. New York, Macmillan, 1932.

6. London, Routledge and Kegan Paul, 1958.

7. For some contemporary examples see David W. McKain (ed.), 'Christianity, Some Non-Christian Appraisals' (New York: McGraw Hill, 1964).

8. 'Das Heilige' (1917), tr. by J. W. Harvey (Oxford University Press, 1923).

9. See his discussion of 'The Two Ways' in Part A, ch. iv, and in Appendices ɪɪ and vɪ.

10. S.C.M. Press, 1960; reprinted as 'World Religions: A Dialogue' (Penguin, 1966).

11. New York University Press, 1965.

12. From 'Deliverance From Error' in W. Montgomery Watt, 'The Faith and Practice of al-Ghazālī' (London: Allen & Unwin, 1963) p. 39.

## CHAPTER 2

1. Kenneth K. S. Ch'en, 'Buddhism, The Light of Asia' (Woodbury, N.Y.: Barron's Educational Series, Inc., 1968) p. 201.

2. See Jaako Hintikka's treatment of Moore's problem ('*p* but I do not believe that *p*') in 'Knowledge and Belief' (Ithaca: Cornell University Press, 1962) pp. 64–78.

3. 'An Empiricist's View of the Nature of Religious Belief' (Cambridge University Press, 1955) pp. 32–3.

4. 'Belief and Loss of Belief: A Discussion', by J. R. Jones and D. Z. Phillips, 'Sophia', vol. ix (March 1970) p. 2. See A. J. Watt, 'Religious Beliefs and Pictures', 'Sophia', vol. ix (Oct. 1970).

CHAPTER 3

1. A. J. Arberry, 'The Koran Interpreted' (London: Allen & Unwin, 1955).

2. See for example E. A. Burtt, 'Types of Religious Philosophy' (New York: Harper, 1951), where in ch. vii he discusses Spinoza and briefly Haeckel under that heading.

3. See William A. Christian, 'Religious Valuations of Scientific Truths', 'American Philosophical Quarterly' vol. 6, no. 2, pp. 144–50 (April 1969).

4. See Paul W. Taylor, 'Normative Discourse' (Prentice-Hall, 1961) on 'ways of life' and 'points of view'. There is the moral point of view, the aesthetic point of view, the religious point of view, the economic point of view, and so on. He construes a way of life as an ordering of points of view. I do not adopt this way of putting the matter, but his discussion is interesting and enlightening.

5. Basil Mitchell (ed.), 'Faith and Logic' (Boston: Beacon Press, 1957) pp. 10–11.

6. 'Religious Language' (London: SCM Press, 1957) and 'Models and Mystery' (London: Oxford University Press, 1964). See William H. Austin, 'Models, Mystery, and Paradox in Ian Ramsey', 'Journal for the Scientific Study of Religion' 7 (1968) pp. 41–55.

7. About why 'believe' would be an unhappy substitute for 'entertain' in this formula see 'Meaning and Truth in Religion', pp. 124–33 on injunctions to believe.

8. Though there can be objections to an act of giving a com-

124

mand. See Nicholas Rescher, 'The Logic of Commands' (London: Routledge & Kegan Paul, New York: Dover Publications, 1966) pp. 16–18.


## CHAPTER 4

1. 'The Varieties of Religious Experience' (New York: Longmans, Green & Co., 1925) p. 340.

2. New York: Harper and Row, 1963.

3. For discussion of an apparent opposition between comprehensive courses of action taught by Buddhism and by Christianity see Masao Abe's review of Paul Tillich, 'Christianity and the Encounter of the World Religions', 'The Eastern Buddhist' (n.s.) vol. I, esp. pp. 120–21.

4. For an interesting study of popular valuations of various religious acts see 'The Ideology of Merit and the Social Correlates of Buddhism in a Thai Village' by S. J. Tambiah in E. R. Leach (ed.), 'Dialectic in Practical Religion' (Cambridge University Press, 1968).

5. Bhikshu Sangharakshita, 'A Survey of Buddhism' (Bangalore: Indian Institute of World Culture, 1966) p. 150.

6. Judah Goldin, 'The Living Talmud' (New York: New American Library, 1957) p. 95.

7. Op. cit., p. 80.


## CHAPTER 5

1. 'An Analysis of Knowledge and Valuation' (La Salle, Illinois: Open Court, 1962) esp. pp. 387–93.

2. 'The Idea of the Holy', p. 5.

3. See, for example, his discussion of the use of ontological terms in mystical religion in 'Reasons and Faiths', pp. 138–40, and his discussion of the role of religion in Indian metaphysics in 'Doctrine and Argument in Indian Philosophy' (London: Allen & Unwin, 1964) ch. x.

4. E.g., G. H. von Wright, 'The Logic of Preference' (Edinburgh University Press, 1963).

5. See J. W. Swanson, 'Religious Discourse and Rational Preference Rankings', 'American Philosophical Quarterly', vol. 4, no. 3 (July 1967).

6. See Gershom G. Scholem's discussions of *devekuth*, which he translates in this way, in 'Major Trends in Jewish Mysticism' (New York: Schocken Books, 1961).

7. 'Japanese Religions' (Kyoto), vol. 4, no. 2, pp. 53, 55 (March 1966).

7a. 'God, Emptiness, and the True Self', in 'The Eastern Buddhist', n.s., vol. ii, no. 2 (November 1969) p. 28.

8. Ibid., p. 30.

9. 'Proslogion', iii, v; tr. M. J. Charlesworth (Oxford: Clarendon Press, 1965).

10. 'The Middle Length Sayings' (Majjhima-Nikāya), tr. I. B. Horner (Pali Text Society) i p. 211.

11. Ibid., p. 212.

12. 'The Questions of King Milinda', tr. T. W. Rhys Davids (Sacred Books of the East) i p. 12.

13. 'An Analysis of Knowledge and Valuation', p. 483. See pp. 494–510.

14. See Lewis, 'Analysis', pp. 521–4.

15. See 'Meaning and Truth in Religion', pp. 156–63.

16. See J. Wach, 'Sociology of Religion' (Chicago: University of Chicago Press, 1944) esp. chs. iv–v; G. van der Leeuw, 'Religion in Essence and Manifestation' (London: Allen & Unwin, 1938) chs. 32–8.


CHAPTER 6

1. For an interesting discussion of the concept of causation in the Pali canon see K. N. Jayatilleke, 'Early Buddhist Theory of Knowledge' (London: Allen & Unwin, 1963) pp. 445 ff.

2. See Jayatilleke, op. cit., pp. 242–3, 281–93, 470–6.

3. Jayatilleke, p. 473, translating from 'Digha Nikaya' i 191 and parallel passages.

4. 'What the Buddha Taught' (New York: Grove Press, 1959) pp. 17–18.

5. A. N. Whitehead, 'Adventures of Ideas' (New York: Macmillan, 1933) p. 221.

6. Edward Conze, 'Buddhist Thought in India' (London: Allen & Unwin, 1962) p. 252.

7. See the discussions by Masao Abe quoted above, pp. 69–70.

8. 'The Central Philosophy of Buddhism' (London: Allen & Unwin, 1960) p. 341.

9. 'A heathen who accepts the seven commandments [enjoined upon Noah] and observes them scrupulously is a "righteous heathen", and will have a portion in the world to come, provided that he accepts them and performs them because the Holy One, blessed be He, commanded them in the Law and made known through Moses, our teacher, that the observance thereof had been enjoined upon the descendants of Noah even before the Law was given.' 'The Code of Maimonides', Book xiv, The Book of Judges, Treatise Five, 8:11, tr. A. M. Hershman (Yale University Press, 1949).

10. E. J. Thomas, 'The History of Buddhist Thought' (London: Routledge & Kegan Paul, 1963) pp. 110–12.

11. Gershom G. Scholem, 'Major Trends in Jewish Mysticism' (New York: Schocken, 1961) p. 283.

CHAPTER 7

1. 'Religion and the Modern Mind' (Philadelphia: Lippincott, 1952) p. 215.

2. The 'Shobogenzo' of Dogen, the Book of Buddhist Sūtras, quoted from 'The Young East' in Phra Khantipalo, 'Tolerance: A Study from Buddhist Sources' (London: Rider & Co., 1964) p. 154.

3. C. I. Lewis, 'Mind and the World Order' (New York: Dover Publications, 1956) p. 35.

# Select Bibliography

Joseph M. Bochenski, O.P., 'The Logic of Religion' (New York: New York University Press, 1965).

William A. Christian, 'Meaning and Truth in Religion' (Princeton: Princeton University Press, 1964).

James Collins, 'The Emergence of Philosophy of Religion' (New Haven: Yale University Press, 1967).

Moses Jung, Swami Nikhilananda, Herbert W. Schneider (eds.), 'Relations among Religions Today, A Handbook of Policies and Principles' (Leiden: E. J. Brill, 1963).

Phra Khantipālo, 'Tolerance, A Study from Buddhist Sources' (London, Rider & Co., 1964).

David W. McKain (ed.), 'Christianity, Some Non-Christian Appraisals' (New York: McGraw-Hill, 1964).

David G. Moses, 'Religious Truth and the Relation between Religions' (Madras: The Christian Literature Society for India, 1950).

Rudolf Otto, 'The Idea of the Holy', tr. J. W. Harvey, 2nd ed. (London: Oxford University Press, 1950).

——, 'Mysticism East and West, A Comparative Analysis of the Nature of Mysticism', tr. B. L. Bracey and Richenda C. Payne (New York: Macmillan, 1932).

Otto Pfleiderer, 'The Philosophy of Religion on the Basis of its History'; Part 1, 'The History of the Philosophy of Religion from Spinoza to the Present Day', 2 vols., tr. A. Stewart and A. Menzies (London: Williams & Norgate, 1886–1887).

Ninian Smart, 'Reasons and Faiths' (London: Routledge & Kegan Paul, 1958).

——, 'World Religions, A Dialogue' (Baltimore: Penguin Books, 1966). (Originally published as 'A Dialogue of Religions', London: SCM Press, 1960.)

Paul W. Taylor, 'Normative Discourse' (Englewood Cliffs, N.J.: Prentice-Hall, 1961).

Paul Tillich, 'Christianity and the Encounter of the World Religions' (New York: Columbia University Press, 1963).
128

# Index